The Women I've Loved

A Dating Diary

By
Ryan LaVoss

Bloomington, IN Milton Keynes, UK

AuthorHouse™
1663 Liberty Drive, Suite 200
Bloomington, IN 47403
www.authorhouse.com
Phone: 1-800-839-8640

AuthorHouse™ UK Ltd.
500 Avebury Boulevard
Central Milton Keynes, MK9 2BE
www.authorhouse.co.uk
Phone: 08001974150

First published by AuthorHouse 1/9/2007

ISBN: 978-1-4259-6506-8 (sc)

Printed in the United States of America
Bloomington, Indiana

This book is printed on acid-free paper.

Table of Contents

Introduction

So who am I to write such a book? I'm just an average guy who somehow happened to either meet or end up in relationships with some of the most wonderful women anywhere. As a result, I feel that I am one of the luckiest men alive. I'm not a user, and I don't get my kicks from telling my life story. These stories are genuine, just like the people they are referring to. Sometimes things worked out. Sometimes they didn't. Some things were nobody's fault. Sometimes I have downright screwed things up myself. Still, fate had a role in other experiences. This book covers over a twenty-five-year span of experiences from good to bad, and right or wrong.

The ride has been great, although I haven't yet "arrived." I have gotten to this point mostly independently, a little dependently, and somewhat vicariously. I long to settle down, but the timing never seems to be right. I tried once before, and the experience was largely responsible for making me the person I am today—a better person.

Each of the five parts in this book is written chronologically, instead of the entire book being in chronological order. As a result, there are literally decades between chapters, in some instances. These women are from all walks of life. Some of them are friends; some are enemies; two of them are sisters; and others, I don't really know how to explain. If variety is truly the spice of life, then I need Maalox.

Maybe you will recognize yourself in this book. I hope your memories are as accurate as mine—be they good, bad, or indifferent. Or, maybe I'm not in your memory at all. However, you all made enough of an impact on my life to inspire this book. You made footprints in the sands of my life. For those of you who are not portrayed in the best light, keep in mind it's only my opinion. Maybe I'm the one who's crazy.

Out of respect for all of you, I have not used your real names. Out of fear of many angry husbands out there, I haven't used mine, either. As a result, I've obviously had to edit the letters that were written before this book was conceived. With the best intentions, here is my tribute to you all.

Part I:
The Women I've Loved

I've loved them all—really. I gave them my best shot. Maybe I didn't express it well enough sometimes. Maybe at other times, I tried too hard. My lifelong journey continues for this elusive thing called love. It has won me and beaten me; made me and molded me. I feel lucky just to have come out alive from all these experiences. At any rate, here's what can happen if you say "yes" to a guy like me.

One of these women taught me that there are different kinds of love. Of course, this is true for the love of parents, siblings, and children. However, there are different kinds of romantic love, also—desperate, idealistic, practical, and sacrificial—to name a few. I've experienced most of them. Maybe there should be a Maslow's Hierarchy pyramid for love. It changes as we grow and as we change ourselves. It changes our lives and our perspective on life. It can even make us vote republican!

Since there are different kinds of love, I also believe that it is possible to love more than one person at a time. Even though, I still maintain that there is only one love of a lifetime. My dearest loved ones, past and present, thank you all for being yourself and for taking a chance. Thank you sincerely for letting me love you and for loving me back, even if for a brief moment in time.

Lip Service

She was the new kid at school—a transfer student. She had lived with her grandmother out of state before she transferred here. It was a good way to get to know her. There's no history, preconceived notions, or expectations. She stood out from the start. She was mature and reserved. She even looked older than her seventeen years. She had a slight lisp that I found endearing. I don't remember exactly how we met, but I think it was in the cafeteria. She had long dark hair and a nice smile. She was a little exotic. I was comfortable around her, probably because of a childhood friend's mature influence. She even had her own apartment, too.

We only dated for a couple of months, I think. I don't remember much about our dates or where we went. However, I did manage to turn her into a Jimmy Buffett fan. On her birthday, I bought her an album, "Havana Daydreaming," and put it in her locker while she was in class. We went "parking" out by the lake a few times. Then one time we were alone at my house. We "explored" a little. It was my first experience, but I still technically remained a virgin. My mother was nice to her. Mom's approval was important to me.

Lip Service was sort of mysterious. I had heard before that women were a mystery, but I had no idea what was in store for me. I offered to take her home from school many times, but she declined. Then one time she said okay, but made me drop her off about a block away. I found out why later on. She finally let me come into her apartment one day. She had admitted to me that she had a roommate. That was fine, but there was a lot of "guy" stuff around. She finally admitted that her roommate was a male. I stood there wide-eyed for a moment while all sorts of visions ran through my head.

Then, unexpectedly, he showed up. Then things quickly took a turn for the worse. I don't remember exactly what was said, but we didn't like each other at all. He asked me who I was, and I said something like, "I'm her boyfriend. Who are you?" That was the wrong thing to say. It turned out her roommate was also her "other" boyfriend—her thirty-two-year-old boyfriend. He asked me to leave. She didn't want me to go. The details are fuzzy, but at some point, he grabbed her by the arm. I grabbed a frying pan. That was another wrong move. Somehow, she intervened, and I made it home in one piece. Needless to say, that put a damper on our relationship. It hurt me deeply that someone could be so deceptive while I was so trusting.

Soon after that, she moved back to her grandmother's house, out of state. For some reason, I wasn't satisfied with the unexpected and unannounced move. As if things weren't obvious enough, I still wanted answers, and set out to get them. Armed with an address and a broken heart, I hopped in the car and drove to grandma's house. A few hours later, I arrived. She was there all right, but something was different about her demeanor.

Then I noticed her ring—her wedding ring. They had eloped and honeymooned at the beach. She was back with her grandmother now because the marriage, only a few weeks' worth, wasn't working out. I guess he grabbed her again or something. She was seeking an annulment. Her grandmother scolded her when she found out I didn't know anything about all of this.

I collected myself and set out for the long drive home. Even my Buffett eight-track tapes didn't help much. I don't think I ever told anyone at school about it. After all, what other seventeen-year-old student could relate to this? This experience stayed with me for years before I ventured into the land of love again. Several years later in my life, this situation would hauntingly repeat itself.

Love on a One-Way Street

We met at a popular, local club at college. She actually asked me to dance first. I was surprised and gladly accepted. She was energetic and lots of fun. We danced until the place closed. They always closed with the same song, *Why Don't We Get Drunk & Screw* by Jimmy Buffett. Earlier, we had also danced to the Stacy Lattisaw version of *Love on a Two Way Street*, which was another popular song at the club. That one would later become my theme song for this relationship.

She was different from your average college student. She was very stylish and sophisticated. She wore outfits with the padded shoulders before they were popular. She wore lots of jewelry and was into designs by Etienne Aigner, who was gaining popularity at the time. She drove a BMW, of course. She had short red hair and drank Moosehead beer. She was toned and tan with smallish perky breasts and a great ass. (My favorite body type to this day.) She was impressive and fascinating. Her life seemed very adventurous. She said she had once taken voice lessons from Beverly Sills. When asked for singing advice, she said Mrs. Sills once told her, "Never sing before breakfast."

She was very popular and always on the move. Scheduling a date with her was a task. She was hard to get a hold of and gone a lot—sometimes for weeks at a time. Then all of a sudden, she would contact me out of the blue. It was frustrating trying to figure out where we stood and where she was half the time. I remember all our dates as being romantic, but I just couldn't quite get the commitment from her that I wanted.

One time I saw her at the club where we had met. She looked so different and uncharacteristic, I didn't recognize her at first. She was wearing a headband and was sporting a sort of Pat Benatar look. She was hanging out with other guys and I saw her kiss one of them. Then she came up to me and said hello, like it was nothing. I thought we had established a relationship by now, but to her, I guess I was just another one of the guys.

I never fully understood her past, or her present for that matter. She had lived in other states and had friends everywhere. Some of them had money, but didn't seem to come from it. Her parents had died and she had a place of her own. Sometimes she stayed with her grandmother. I don't know how or if she ever finished college.

One time during Christmas break, I was working in my home town. She was supposedly out of state and I hadn't heard from her in awhile. Then she just walked back into my life during one afternoon at work. How excited I was to see her! So we made plans for dinner that night. I took her to my home and introduced her to my parents. She was dressed in a stylish and expensive lavender outfit with padded shoulders. I was so enamored with her. Each time I saw her, I would fall in love all over again. We went to a nice restaurant and it was there that I gave her a gift. It was a gold Aigner watch in the shape of the designer's insignia. It was rare and unique, just like her. She loved it.

Sometime after that, we planned a big date. Bob Fosse's, "Dancing" was on tour in the area so I bought tickets. I picked her up at her house. She looked so beautiful. We had dinner at the nicest place in town to eat, located on top of what was the tallest building in the city at the time. It was incredibly romantic. I had obviously fallen for her before this date, but there was no turning back now. We dined on the finest steak and wine. After attempting to cut her steak with the only knife on the table—a butter knife—she asked the waiter for a steak knife.

"That IS your steak knife," he replied.

"Oh," she said.

Then we both laughed for awhile over the incident. Afterwards, it was off to the show.

I got lost and we had to stop at a fast food drive-through for directions. The show was great, and we had good seats. The drive back home was long, and she slept most of the way. I played my favorite songs on tape and sang to her while she slept. By the time we got back to her place, it was very late. I planned to wake her with a kiss, but when I pulled into the driveway, the rocking motion of the car woke her up. So much for that idea, but it was still the best date I had ever had at that point. I escorted her into her house and we kissed good-night. It was the first time I had experienced love this deeply. I wanted her to be my first in every way.

Then she disappeared again for a long time. I didn't see her for a couple of months. I had been asking around about her, and found out some of her "friends" were supposedly dealing drugs. I think it was her grandmother who told me she was back in Florida. About that same time, my best friend and I had been planning a road trip to visit some friends down there. So I figured I'd kill two birds with one stone, and go looking for her since we were going to be in a town close by. We made the trip and had a great time visiting, but my mind was only on her. Once again, I wanted answers and set out to get them. Gee, this pattern sounds familiar, doesn't it?

So off I went one evening to find her. I went to the town where she had formerly been living, thinking she might be back there. The whole atmosphere was different. It was like "Miami Vice" before that show was aired. The complex I thought she had lived at was secured and I couldn't get in. So I hung out for awhile and started asking people coming and going if they knew her. They weren't very friendly and I soon realized I wasn't welcome there, so I left. Still without answers, I was only more frustrated. Later, I learned that town had a unique nickname, "Mafia" Marco Island.

I caught up with her a couple of months later at her grandmother's house. It was awkward. She told me about some guys she had dated during our relationship. She admitted some of them had been dealing drugs. She had also given away her BMW to some guy in Florida, and now she was suddenly joining the air force. She was due to ship out to California soon. I was devastated. How could I have done it again? Why was I drawn to these mysterious women who didn't have normal lives? I thought about her every day for years.

Then, several years later, she looked me up and somehow contacted me. She was going to be back in my state and we decided to meet. Could I finally get some closure? I was shocked when I saw her. She was a totally different person. She had multiple earrings, and maybe a tattoo; I don't remember exactly. Her hair and clothes were sort of "punk" style. She had definitely been in California too long. She didn't appeal to me at all.

She had done well in the military and advanced in rank. She told me she had also been married and divorced. I couldn't believe it. I managed to tell her I regretted not losing my virginity to her. She reassured me that it wasn't meant to be. I think somehow she was trying to protect me from getting hurt even worse. We parted with a hug and wished each other well. I didn't think about her much after that. It was good to have my idealistic image of her brought down to earth. At least I had gotten my closure this time.

Forget Newport

We were on our way to Newport one summer weekend to visit my best friend's girlfriend. We flew into Boston for the day and planned to drive over the next day. We hung out, shopped at Filene's Basement, and grabbed dinner at Legal Seafood. Later that night, we went bar hopping. Our first stop was the famous "Bull & Finch" bar. There was a beautiful woman among the crowd with long blonde hair who stood head and shoulders above everyone else. Her height and beauty were quite imposing. I looked around and all the guys were looking at her, but nobody made a move. After about a half hour of this, I decided to fire the first shot. After all, I was a tourist and no one would ever see me again, right?

I mustered the determination and marched up to her. To the best of my memory, the conversation went something like this:

"Do you realize that most men are intimidated by you?"

"Really?" she replied.

"Yea, but I want you to know you don't intimidate me," I said.

"Why not?" she asked.

Then I said something brilliant.

"Because I've had two drinks!"

She lost interest soon afterwards. Imagine that. I slithered back to my corner, and many of the guys were staring at me. I guess they saw me get shot down and figured they'd better come up with something better than whatever I had said or the same would happen to them. Not only did I blow my chances with her, but I also blew her chances with some of the other guys that night. I'm sure she had nothing to worry about, though.

We went to another club after that. I don't remember the name of the place we were in, but we danced with some local girls. Across the room I noticed a very thin girl with short brown hair. She had big brown eyes and a sweet, innocent look about her. I walked over and asked her to dance. She accepted and we shook our booties out on the floor for awhile. I thanked her afterwards, and we talked for awhile. Then we separated and went back to our friends. Sometime later, she and her friend were about to leave for the night, so she came back over to tell me she enjoyed meeting me. I obliged and suggested we could meet again the next day before we went out of town. She said okay, and we agreed on a meeting place.

Meanwhile, my friend had met someone whom he was interested in, and they wanted to see each other again, too. The next day came and we decided we wanted to meet our new friends instead of going to Newport. There was no love lost between him and his girlfriend.

She was very nice and had an honesty about her that was appealing. We went our separate ways after lunch, and we agreed to meet again, if possible. When it was time to fly home, my friend got bumped from the flight. We flipped a coin and I won. So I flew home while he spent the night at Logan. I called her over the next few weeks and we planned to meet again. So I flew back for a weekend. She picked me up and we toured the town. We had a nice time together and got along well. After dinner, we walked around Nathaniel Square. Then she showed me the building where she worked.

On the top floor of that building was a place called the Harvard Club. She somehow had a pass code or keys—I can't remember which. It was closed that evening for some reason, but she took me in to show me around. It was completely dark. We went over to the full-length windows and gazed out. The Queen Elizabeth II was docked in the bay, and some formal event was taking place aboard. I figured if she could get us in the Harvard Club, she could get us onto the QE II, but that was asking a bit too much. Besides, I didn't have a tux. She was such a sweet person and the setting was irresistible. I took her into my arms and we kissed by the windows overlooking the city lights, the bay, and the QEII. Eat your hearts out, guys! I was feeling pretty good by the time we got back on the elevator. It was time to return to her place.

As we made out on her couch, my hand began to wander, and wander, and wander. Poor thing, she was so flat-chested, I couldn't find her breasts! I discreetly tried to look without disrupting the moment or embarrassing her. Finally, I stood up and reached out my hand for hers, and we went arm-in-arm into the bedroom. Now with her clothes off, I had landmarks. She was sweet and caring. We made innocent love, as if we were saying hello and goodbye simultaneously. It was meaningful and memorable. She even called out my name as she climaxed. That simple gesture bridged the gap between us from friends to lovers. We were now connected physically and emotionally.

The next morning as she got dressed, I took a closer look around her apartment. Glancing over the books on her shelves, I became aware of her Jewish heritage. Although it didn't matter to me, I sensed that this might be an obstacle for a serious relationship. Distance, of course, was the main barrier. I still wanted to make the most of it, since the weekend had gone well, so far.

As she drove me back to the airport, I tried to talk her into coming to see me for my birthday, which was about a month away. She avoided making any commitment. As we pulled up to the terminal, she was still beating around the bush.

So I finally said, "Shut up and kiss me!"

She did, and then we said our goodbyes. It would be the last time I would see her.

I wrote her a letter when I got home, explaining how much I wanted to see her again. As the meeting date we had set grew closer, she finally called and explained that she wouldn't be coming. Just like her flight, our relationship would never get off the ground. Thank goodness there's always someone in most relationships with common sense. I decided after that experience that I would not do this with anyone else. One-night stands were just not what they're cracked up to be. It's usually someone's feelings that get cracked up.

Beacon

I remember the first time I saw her. She was facing away from me. All I saw was this hair—her gorgeous hair. It was *alive.* I just stood there, paralyzed with fascination. People were around me, but I wasn't aware of them. Then after a moment, she turned around, and my life changed. *And the angels danced!*

We were one when we danced. I remember one instance in particular, at our beautiful home. It was the holiday season. The ruby stemware on the dining table glowed softly. There were multi-colored reflections from the crystal in the curio, and the angles danced with us! I could *feel* their presence. When I look back on this memory, it's as if I am looking down on it from up above—a view from their perspective.

Only God loved her more than I did. Even though He knew how it would end, I'm sure He was pleased with the way we loved each other. It was truly unselfish and truly unconditional during those special moments. It was as if we somehow transcended human love, with our souls briefly joining the ebb and flow of heaven. Could they have been recorded in eternity? Is that our contribution to heaven? There's nothing to show for it here on earth except words that could only be imagined in translation.

The angels are gone now. I haven't felt them since. I miss them. They carried us. I need them now. My soul still weeps, what's left of it. Are the angels weeping, too? I don't know how to un-change my life. I didn't learn how to love. I didn't even have to try. It was unleashed from my soul the moment I met her. It taught me why and how to live.

Now I just exist; a shell of a man. She drained all the life out of me, like a black widow spider. I was left as the dangling carcass in

11

her web. Time has healed nothing. Not just the love, but everything. The tangible and intangible composition of our lives simply can't be recreated. How could it have been so right, yet not meant to be? How do you fail at love?

Will I just go through the motions of life and of marriage? What do I have left to give? Hope truly springs eternal. Someday I will have the answers. I would trade them for the feeling again if I could. And the angels still dance; *for someday, I will join them again.*

Those were my feelings at the time. I could have written a whole book about her. As you have gathered, it was no ordinary love, but a once-in-a-lifetime love. I even got a second chance, but it wasn't meant to be. There are a hundred stories I could share, but that's not what this chapter is about. I remember the exact date and time we started dating, and the same for our breakups. Like Gloria Vanderbilt said, "The phone can ring and your whole life can change in a blink." For me, that phone call came at 2:20 p.m. on Friday, August 17, 2001. The following story is one of our more memorable events during the course of our relationship.

There was the time we went out for New Year's Eve. Anticipating a memorable evening, we eagerly dressed up for the occasion. We went to one of the best restaurants in town—my personal favorite. Sparing no expense, we dined on lobster and champagne. After a near perfect dinner by candlelight, my credit card was returned. It had expired that day. Luckily, she had enough cash on her to pay for the meal, which wasn't cheap.

After profuse apologies and promises of repayment the next day, we went to get into the car. It was raining. I then discovered I had locked the keys in her car. The spare key was back at home.

After some debate, we decided to take our only option. Fortunately, we didn't live far from the restaurant. So we walked home in the cold rain, in the dark, in our best attire, on New Year's Eve. That's true love.

We ended up at her parent's house after retrieving the car. When we told them about our adventure, all we could do was just laugh about it. They took pictures of us that night. They turned out to be the best photos that were ever made of us.

The following are some of the actual love letters that I sent to her during the course of our relationship. The first letter was written after a whirlwind couple of months together. We had just broken up for the first time. Despite my burnout, I still realized how special she was, as you will see. It was written in lavender, her favorite color (besides periwinkle blue). I hope someone out there loves someone this much.

My Dearest,

Now that my world has stopped spinning, I wanted to share some reflections with you. I write this letter, as I have lain awake yet another night hopelessly anticipating your call. I believe that our relationship went way too far, too fast. We were trying to make decisions that were too big, too soon. I didn't have time to process the aspects of each issue before yet another was presented. Our lives have different levels of complexity. If I could give you any advice for future relationships, it would be to slow down a bit.

I also believe that our timing was off. Maybe if we had met earlier in our lives or later, things could have been different. We are both too unstable right now to sustain a relationship. We have both had many changes in our lives recently, from careers to different lifestyles than what we were used to in the past.

I truly do want to remain friends, if possible. One thing I know about you is that you don't go back to anyone. You only move forward. That's one quality I admire about you. Whenever I see you from now on, no matter how strong I am on the outside, my heart will cry out for you on the inside.

Whomever I may meet in the future, she will not have all of my heart because there will always be a part of it embedded within you. I hope you haven't cried much for me. I've done enough of that for both of us.

I know great things are in store for you. Your ambition and talents are incredible. Even though I didn't call you by it, my pet name for you was Beacon. You stand out among the rest. People are drawn to you. Life itself is drawn to you, and you live it for all it's worth. You live each day to the fullest, and you are rewarded for it. I have learned from your examples and your advice.

Among the many things I am thankful for because of knowing you, here are but a few:
Never have I seen such beauty as that possessed by you.
Never have I touched skin so soft as yours.
Never have I experienced such passion as that which exudes from your soul.
There are so many people in this world who could love you, but I am among the few who were loved in return by you. That is the greatest gift from you that I treasure.

As for the regrets:
Never will a white, horse-drawn carriage await us.
Never will a child breathe life from our consummation.
And never will our love be greater than our differences.

I will close now, having expressed my thoughts and feelings with you. I will continue to pray for you.

All my love,

We stayed in touch as friends over the next several months. During that time, she was dating another man. He had more money than me, but I had more "inches." What a tough decision that must have been for her! The second note was handwritten in a Christmas card. I still gave her presents that year, even though we weren't dating. This was my way of gallantly vowing to win her back. She cried.

My Dearest & Most Beautiful Friend,

I can't express my gratefulness enough to you for being a part of my life. Knowing you has touched my heart and soul unlike any other. Please accept my gifts as appreciation for a relationship still shared together as friends.

You have said before that you don't really know what love is. So my Christmas wish for you is that someday God will reveal to you what true love really is. Although you saw it on my face a hundred times, I hope someday you can experience the feeling for yourself.

It truly is better to have loved and lost than to never have loved at all. It will change your life for the better. Maybe knowing that can help remove any fears or doubts you may have about it. Thank you and may next year be more fulfilling for you than this one.

The Last Man Standing

The next letter was written after we reunited on Valentine's day. During that incredible year, we lived, we loved, we laughed, we learned, and we left a legacy for others to follow.

My Dearest,

You have asked me to list the things I admire about you and the reasons why I love you. Here is my best attempt. This list can never diminish, but can only grow. It is one way of thanking you for all that you are and all that you do.

Abilities:
Your talents are amazing. I love your musical abilities; they are an expression of your soul. Your French language skills make you exotic and romantic. Your singing talent (yes, I've heard you sing!) is mesmerizing. Your distinctive taste and style are an extension of your creative finesse. Your cooking is an expression of your love for others. Your classic clothing style commands respect and admiration. You have a natural talent for teaching, and what a wonderful way to give back to others! All your students will fondly remember you.

Accomplishments:
You have accomplished more so far than many people do in their whole lives. Your level of education and training has earned you countless awards and recognition. You are driven to do your best in every career you have chosen. You have always accomplished and you always will. You don't know any other way.

Ambition:
Once you set a goal for yourself, you are driven to it. The word "No" isn't in your vocabulary when it comes to challenges. You can do anything you set your mind to. That's why you

will be an excellent realtor or whatever else you choose to do. The world is yours!

Appreciation:
Your appreciation of others and the things they do for you is unselfish and sincere. You are so easy to please in many ways. You get so excited over simple things and that makes others feel good. Thank you for making the little things count.

Beauty:
There are no words to describe your beauty. God truly molded you after his angels. My eyes will never tire of you.

Belief in me:
Your encouragement has meant a lot to me. You have been very patient with me in this area. Thank you for trying to bring out the best in me. You can see good things in me that sometimes I don't see myself. I won't disappoint you.

Confidence:
You present yourself to others with positive confidence. You handle situations deftly and with persistence until you get the desired outcome. Things work out for you because you determine that they will.

Devotion:
You are a devoted and loyal friend, partner, and mother. Most of your friends are for keeps. Time doesn't dissolve relationships easily for you. You have a nurturing spirit that bonds others to you. You leave others feeling better about themselves than they did before they met you.

Intellect

You have the skills to converse with anyone in any situation. Your diverse background enables you to objectively evaluate subjects presented before you. Your intelligence is intriguing and captivating. You interact instead of react. Like someone once said, you have a response for everything.

Laughter

Like a child full of life, your laughter is unbridled and contagious. The sheer joy of your happiness bursts forth unabashed from the heart. Thank you for making the world a brighter place.

Love of life

Like I have said before, you seem to live life to the fullest. You have a desire to experience all that life has to offer. You embrace the world around you with an unquenched zest. The wide range of god's creatures you love and respect is admirable. You appreciate all forms of life whether they are plants or animals, and I'm sure they love you back. Like a beautiful Beacon, you have drawn me irretrievably into your heart, safe from the stormy seas. Your love for me is more than I could ever deserve. I pray each day that our lives were meant to be together forever.

Passion

This one is ours alone, never to diminish. Thank you, my love.

Patience

You have been extraordinarily patient with me. You must see beyond the surface to a greater good. My deepest appreciation for your forgiveness has been and will continue to be expressed through my commitment to you.

Personality

What fun you are to be around! Life is just a blast with you. You can somehow turn little things into a memorable adventure. Your unpredictability is never anticipated.

And then there's the little girl inside who occasionally shows her vulnerability. How endearing she is. Then it's my turn to nurture and protect her as a father would to the daughter he never had.

Softness

How soft you are! Holding you is soothing and comforting unlike anyone that has ever graced my arms. Holding you is therapy for my soul.

Spirituality

God is in the center of your life and provides you with moral direction. No matter how busy your day has been, you make time for the truth and the word. You are an example for myself and others to follow.

Finally, I love that special way you look at me. It is with complete trust and love. No words or actions are necessary. I stop wondering how or why; I just know we were meant to be. It's a simple understanding that no matter what, we are there for each other.

These are the reasons why I love you, my dearest. Please remember them, for they are not merely words. They are all part of who you are, and won't ever change. And neither will my love for you.

Sincerely,

Finally, there came the last letter. It was written in blue, to reflect my mood and to signify its distinction from the others. After lengthy discussions about our compatibility, we mutually agreed it wouldn't work. Ironically, this occurred after an incredibly romantic Valentine's day the following year. Sometimes love just isn't enough. Fate dealt its hand, and she eventually got married without me.

Dear,

Okay, I had to write just one more time—the last letter from the last man standing. Not that it will change anything, but it may help bring closure to this chapter of my life. I'll still leave a light on for you, though.

I feel as though I have fulfilled one of my purposes in life—to completely give myself and my soul to another. I loved you as much as a man can possibly love a woman. No matter how long I live, where I am, what I accomplish, or whom I may marry, one of my last breaths on this earth will utter your name. I have no regrets. Perhaps you will find some comfort and solace in knowing that you will always be loved.

Every time I saw you, my heart skipped a beat. Now it doesn't beat at all. My blood must be circulating by gravity. I miss you desperately. Oh to feel you once more. Oh to see your hair glow with sunlight again. Oh to experience your laughter...

And oh, how we danced! Anywhere and everywhere we had the chance! Pure magic! How I will treasure those moments, never to be duplicated with anyone else! Those were our unspoken vows, which can never be broken! So much for "no public displays of affection," huh?

So many things about you are irreplaceable. Why did you have to be so beautiful, so soft, and so irresistible? Why couldn't you be like any other woman I would have gotten over by now? Why have you affected my life so profoundly? Why are you so damned impossible? That's my girl!

You have shown me the tools I need to succeed in life, and out of respect for you, I will use them. My beautiful Beacon, by giving me so much support and encouragement, you will positively impact others through me.

I know I have affected you also. We couldn't have lasted as long as we did without influencing each other's lives. Deep down inside, I hope I'm that doubt in the back of your mind about your future relationships. We always joked that someday if we turn 50 and are not attached, we would revisit the possibility of a future together. I hope you were serious, because I sure was. Until then, I guess Z-2 will have to do.

It is with heartfelt sincerity that I express my appreciation for our time together. No, it wasn't perfect, but my love for you was. I accepted our differences, at the cost of my humility. I feel as though I have let everyone down because I wasn't able to take better care of you. That task is now in God's hands.

Someone once said, "Life is determined not by what we have lost but what we have left." I'm so rich for knowing you; so poor for losing you. I guess we all do the best we can. Forever you will be a light that guides me, and the anguish that haunts me.

As always, my thoughts and prayers are with you.

Sincerely,

As I look back on these letters now, I view them not as a tragedy, but as testimony that love is *real* and it is *out there*. Shouldn't you do the same before you settle for security, convenience, or anything less than you deserve?

BARBIE

She was the one who got away. She was simply "The One." What, you ask? How could anyone top Beacon? Well, that depends on my perspective, which was different now. Barbie was such a proud woman. She was tall, shapely, and utterly beautiful. She was the very essence of a woman. Her shoulder-length blonde hair was always perfectly styled, and her taste in clothing was classy and conservative. I was instantly attracted to her. A mutual friend and neighbor, Genius, introduced us. (She has her own chapter later on.) I was new to the neighborhood, and the three of us began to visit as friends. We all lived within fifty feet of each other. Barbie and I had some disagreements right from the start. We both took a strong stand on certain issues. She thought I was an asshole. I was still bitter over Beacon and cynical about women in general. Barbie was strong-willed, intelligent, and very independent. Well, she could just buy her own damned hotdog, thank you!

Then one evening, Genius and I were out on the town and called Barbie to come join us. She did and we had a good time. Barbie had to lean in close to talk over the band. That's when the barrier began to come down. It was intensely tempting to be so close to her—cheek-to-cheek—and not touch her. Our disagreements aside, I enjoyed being close to her. Her hair tickled my face and her perfume teased my senses. I just wanted to grab her and kiss her, but I feared I would get slapped. She was not the kind of woman to mess with like that.

We left there and went to another place close by. It was "March Madness" and the games were on. She was a big Duke fan, and I wasn't. It was a friendly disagreement for a change. So I mustered the courage to make a bet with her on the game. If Duke won, I'd buy her dinner; and if they lost, she had to buy me dinner. To my disbelief, she agreed. It must have been the wine or something. What a win-win bet! To my delight, Duke lost. (That's *always* a delight). She was very busy and couldn't honor the bet until about two or three weeks later. I was expecting her to find an excuse to back out, but she didn't. So the date was set and out we went. She even picked me up in her car. It was a little intimidating. She drove a Porsche that she referred to as her "penis compensator." I pondered over whether or not to actually let her pay for dinner.

I was a little nervous at first. Okay, a lot nervous, but I began to feel comfortable soon after. There were no disagreements this time. Everything she said made her even more attractive to me. We discussed our commonalities instead of our differences. True to her word, she paid for dinner. However, as she started to pay the waitress, I stopped her hand and said I would let her pay only on one condition—that I would pay the next time. She accepted, and we agreed to another dinner the next week. Meanwhile, back at my place, I asked her for a kiss goodnight. She said okay, but it was quick and awkward. I remember thinking, "Boy, she'll have to do better than that!" I later learned that she was very nervous also.

For the next date, I dressed to kill. She always dressed so classy and carried herself like a lady. It was on this second dinner date that she grew to become a part of me. We discussed the important questions for hours. I kept thinking, "When is she going to mess up? When is she going to say or do the wrong thing?" She never did. Her answers kept racking up checkmarks. She had the values and character I was looking for. I loved everything about her. And before the night was over, I would love her heart, too.

I remember when it hit me. It was about halfway through dinner when I looked at her and realized that her inner beauty even exceeded her outer beauty. It's one of those rare moments when the outside world fades away and you exist with her as one in the universe. I think we may have been the last ones to leave the restaurant. Before we got out of the car back at home, I held her hand and told her I would have no trouble committing to an exclusive relationship with her. She agreed. Later, as we said goodnight by the door, I just looked at her and my eyes began to water.

"Oh Barbie," I said, and then I couldn't say anymore.

She looked at me, with her eyes watering also, and said, "Say it."

So I did. "I'm falling in love with you," I said.

She said she was also falling for me. We embraced and helplessly cried on each other's shoulders for a few moments. After regaining our composure, we were able to say goodnight. That kiss was MUCH better than the first one!

She praised me more than any other girlfriend ever had before. She told her family and friends that I was "almost perfect." She thought I was handsome and told me so. She repeatedly told me, "You're so much of a man," and "You're all that and a bag of chips!"

She was so good to me. I loved her family, and mine loved her. It was almost too good to be true.

The next couple of months were a whirlwind. I needed her in so many ways. She encouraged me and advised me. There was so much to learn from her. We conversed intellectually one moment and childlike the next. She made me laugh out loud, contemplate my life, and dare to dream. She had been the consummate professional, wife, and mother. Our love was realistic and practical, while being fun and romantic at the same time. She was firm, yet forgiving. We dreamed of how wonderful our life could be together. Yes, there are different kinds of love. I now understood that.

She took good care of herself. She worked out at the gym, ate right, and had more energy than me. She said her figure matched the shape of a Barbie doll, hence her nickname for this chapter. She was the type of woman you would want to take ballroom dance lessons with, and I gladly would have. She had the longest and most perfectly shaped legs I had ever seen. I used to hold them one at a time in my hands and would begin to kiss and caress them. Starting at her ankles, I would slowly kiss and lick my way up to the top of her thighs, savoring every moment of it, as did she.

She would say things to me like, "I'll give you all night long to stop that." As much as we wanted each other, we were good about not getting too carried away. She wanted to wait until we were "official", and I respected her wishes.

One of my favorite things to do was to leave her surprises around town. I went to the nail shop where she got her manicures and left her a gift certificate for a free session. I did the same at her favorite restaurant, where she frequently stopped by on her way home from work. It took her a couple of months to discover all my little "surprises." I loved getting the responses from her. It added a little adventure to our relationship. She was so appreciative of everything I did for her; it made me want to do even more.

Although the thought of it terrified me, we discussed marriage. With the exception of an age difference, there was no other reason not to marry her. I dwelled on it daily and dreamt of it nightly. That's probably what scared me the most. She was so *right*. I had even planned out how I would have proposed to her.

Then one day she found the lump. The following sonogram and biopsy confirmed cancer. Soon after came the news of surgery. She had to have a mastectomy. It was like being in a wreck in slow motion. I feared for her life. A few days later, she had an important discussion with me. Under the circumstances, she decided that she wanted to reveal herself to me. I understood how difficult that must have been for her. Once she did, there was no turning back. It was nothing short of beautiful; the way love is supposed to be expressed. We were one when we were together.

I was there with her family when they wheeled her out of surgery. Only semi-conscious, she was worried about her lipstick. Right then and there, I knew she was going to be fine.

Long months of chemo and another mastectomy followed. She lost her hair, but not her dignity. I have *never* witnessed such a display of faith and courage. Cancer had picked the wrong person to mess with this time. The cancer itself became the victim. I did everything I could for her, but her stubborn independence limited my efforts.

Between her and her mother, who was also just as stubborn, about all I could do was "shut up and eat." (An inside joke; you had to be there.) I shaved my head bald in a show of support.

Then along came something I couldn't compete with—the past. About halfway through her chemotherapy, her ex came back to reconcile. He decided it was time to dump his girlfriend and try to act like a husband again. She was legally separated while we had dated, but I was no match against twenty years of marriage. Still, I resented the fact that she was asked to make such a big decision under such duress. After all, she wasn't good enough for him when she was healthy, so why would he want to take on this burden now? In a different perspective, her husband was equally damned if he did and damned if he didn't. Who am I to question his motives? I also guess familiarity seemed more comforting to her during this time of her life-changing issues. Again, there was nothing I could do.

As we said goodbye for the last time, the radio in her home was on as usual. However, this time, for reasons unknown, it was not on a country station that she so loved, but a different one. The song, *Into the Night* played as we said goodbye for the last time at the same doorway where we had declared our love just a few months earlier. Like I did almost every night before, I walked home. This time, however, I didn't look back. She waited and watched by the door as always, but I just kept walking.

All of a sudden, I had lost my love, my best friend, and life as I knew it. Our lives unraveled like leaves in the wind. Ahead for me, I experienced months of sleepless heartache, on top of worrying about her health. How many more times could I go through this? What would I ever have left to offer anyone else?

She fully recovered and life has moved on, leaving us in its wake. Her husband never did figure out who I was, even though we were close neighbors until I moved away several months later. I ran into her only a few times after our breakup. We were polite but short-spoken. It tore both of us up. Her birthday came a few months later. As wrong as it was, I sent her presents and flowers—dozens of flowers. There were enough to equal her age. The card read, "There's one for each year you have graced this earth!" The presents were more practical things that she needed. I had them delivered to her at work, of course. I could *feel* her reaction. Yes, the feelings were still there. I just wanted to emphasize them. I later heard that she cried all day long. Since then, I have respected the fact that she is a married woman.

Life is fragile and unpredictable. It can be great one moment and not the next; like the time I stalled her Porsche out on the busiest street in town. I guess that was sort of a foreshadowing of things to come. Yes, I wrote her love letters, too. I will share one of them with you.

They were different from that ones I had written to Beacon. I didn't have to plead for Barbie's love. I didn't have to ask or do anything to earn it. Her love was simply there for me. My love felt more secure with her than with Beacon, who was more unpredictable. By comparison, my love for Beacon was desperately insecure. Every man wanted her and she knew it, and used it to her advantage. I didn't know how to compete with them. I just thought if I loved her enough, then everything would be all right.

However, Barbie had unwavering integrity, character, and faith. She simply met my expectation of what love is all about. She loved me like I had always wanted to be loved. Yes, we actually had some disagreements, and this letter was written after one of them. Barbie, just remember that no matter what, or no matter when, I'll be here for you—if only as a friend, or if only in my prayers.

Dear,

This poor house key is confused. It may need counseling. I know how it feels. I think the best thing for you right now is time. No amount of it can change my feelings for you. There are many reasons we are so compatible—just a reminder for future reference.

You meet my expectations of what love is all about. I love the way you love me. It is kind, caring, nurturing, compassionate, and sincere. You meet my expectations of how people should live their lives—honestly, faithfully, hard working, cleanly, self respectfully, and with a good dose of humor.

Our values, morals, and principles are closely matched. I admire and respect your intelligence. We dress so well together. We communicate with understanding. (Well, most of the time!) You fit so well into my arms. And <u>wow</u>, what legs! You would truly be a life companion in every sense of the word.

I thought my heart had finally healed. How foolish of me to think I could end up with someone as wonderful as you. Thank you for showing me what true love is all about. I can rest assured with that. I will hold our memories steadfast, along with my hope. I don't give up easily, especially for something worth waiting for.

You have chosen a love filled with doubt instead of one filled with hope. Still, I wish you all the best in health, life, and love. Maybe someone else will be holding your hand during chemo and surgery, but I'll be holding your heart. My thoughts and prayers are with you.

My love now and forever,

Part II:
The Women I've Dated

Some of you will be surprised to be in this category. Others will be disappointed. Most of you were my girlfriends, and some of you were definitely not. So, some of you have every right to claim that I was never your boyfriend. Therefore in this section, I've considered "dated" to mean more than one date, as in two. Even some of those were just lunch dates, but it helps distinguish this section from the next.

Even so, these women made a lasting impression on me in one way or another. I cared for them all, or at least I tried to, if I had enough of a chance. Most of these memories are filled with fun and fancy, until I got dumped. They helped define me as a boyfriend and developed me as a man. The laughter and tears were worth it all. I'm glad all of them were part of my life and wish all of them well.

No Hanky Panky

Back in high school again, round two. She was the little red-haired girl and I was Charlie Brown. We were completely different. She was smart, focused, and disciplined. I was basically the class clown. The only thing we had in common was athletics. She was on the swim team. I was on the tennis team. I remember trying to study with her, but I couldn't keep up. The highlight of our relationship was going to the prom, and I don't remember most of that. I was mostly worried about scratching my dad's Cadillac.

This one lasted about as long as my first girlfriend, Lip Service. In a determined effort to make it last longer this time, I gave her a ring about six weeks into our relationship. It was a simple going steady ring, but it was enough to scare her away. At least there wasn't any drama or mysterious unanswered questions. This girl was as straight as they come.

When she broke up with me, I remember going out to my car and sitting there for a couple of hours listening to music for stress relief. I got into trouble the next day for missing a couple of classes. I remember trying to figure out this ritual called dating. I figured that for some reason, I wasn't much of a boyfriend. That mindset stayed with me for many years to come.

The Mole

Okay, this one I have to include for prosperity's sake, although I'd rather have left her out. At one point in-between colleges, I ended up temporarily in a small rural town in another state. I had one good friend there, but that was about it. I didn't have much in common with most of the other people there. I don't remember exactly how I met her, but somehow I became infatuated with this girl. She was sweet, simple, and rough around the edges. I knew from the start that there was no serious future, but she was crazy about me, and I liked the attention. It made me feel wanted and more confident. There wasn't much to do in that town, so we hung out and drove around listening to Barry Manilow tapes.

We eventually began fooling around. Being sexually inexperienced and not staying in town for long, I figured this was my best chance. Don't get me wrong. I was caring and affectionate, but there wasn't true love, either. At least we were committed to each other. One time we were in her room fooling around. Privacy was an issue, being in a dorm room and all. So the clothes stayed on. She took me to the point of no return, but that caused another problem. I couldn't walk out into a lobby and across campus with this obvious "stain" on my jeans. So I went to the bathroom and began trying to clean myself up. I got the idea to wet a washcloth and wipe off my pants. This left an even bigger wet spot. Right about this time, her roommate came back and suddenly walked in on me while I was blow-drying this huge spot on my jeans. She laughed, and I turned red. Oh well, chalk that one up for experience. After that, the roommate kidded me about the "blow job" I gave myself.

Then there was the mole. One day we drove to a nearby park by a lake. We were sitting on a picnic bench, eating some snacks. No one was around, so we decided to start snacking on other things. As our sexuality progressed, I boldly unbuttoned her blouse. She was wearing a front snap bra. She had to unhook it for me. Her breasts were huge. As I began to go down on one of them, I noticed a mole next to her nipple. Undeterred, I took it in my mouth. After several enjoyable minutes for both of us, I eagerly went to work on the other one. As I pulled away, I noticed that the "mole" was missing! A sinking feeling grew in the pit of my stomach as I realized it wasn't a mole after all. Even worse, I had swallowed whatever it was. I didn't say anything to her about it. Like I said, she was rough around the edges.

I decided to treat her like a lady, leading up to the big "event." The budding romantic began to come out in me. If I made a mistake, she wouldn't know the difference. We planned for the "big night." It would be on the weekend of her birthday. I made reservations for a suite at a posh hotel in the capital city, which was a couple of hours away. I even bought her a nice dress to wear for the event.

The weekend before, she took me to her home in an even more rural farm town. It was then that I realized how different we were. Her mother took apart the new dress I bought her and re-sewed it to make more room for the bust. That unnerved me, to see an expensive dress torn apart like that. I soon recovered by eating some strawberry pie her mother had made for me. Later that afternoon, her mother had to leave for some reason, and that left us alone for awhile. One thing led to another and we ended up in her bed.

So much for the big plans we had made for the next weekend. She was on the pill, so the stage was set. She also said she had a tipped uterus. I didn't know what the hell that meant, but it sure sounded like she was safe to me. It was a nice experience, but hurried and a little awkward. I remember the exact date and time. I got that "tingling" feeling all over, but there wasn't much time to bask in the afterglow. I was nearly twenty-three when I lost my virginity.

The next day we had dinner with the family and all the relatives after church. (I remember *not* repenting.) I felt like I was on display or something, by the way everyone was fawning over me. I got suspicious when the preacher showed up for dinner, too. I was sitting at one end of the table. I looked up at one point, about halfway through my meal, and everyone had finished and they were all staring at me. They ate like hogs, and were waiting for me to finish so they could all dive in for dessert. Then someone asked me when we were getting married. Now I was angry, but I didn't show it. I felt like I had been set up. I calmly but firmly had to tell them that it probably wasn't going to happen. What on earth had she told them about me? I simply couldn't relate with her upbringing, and our futures were on two completely different paths. Nonetheless, I felt it was too late to cancel our plans for the next weekend.

So off we went to the big city for our romantic weekend. It wasn't so romantic and I felt guilty for going through with it. I was strengthening a bond in her mind that was only weakening in mine. I would be leaving town soon and this was my way of saying thank you and goodbye.

I remember going down on her in the shower, or at least trying to do so. I gagged. Maybe this sex stuff wasn't what it was cracked up to be after all. I had tried to wait for the right circumstances and relationship, but it still didn't feel appropriate. We drove back the next day. I knew I had just made things worse.

Then at some point she decided to tell me about her "secret gift." She could "know" things about current or future events. A "little black cloud" would come and tell her things. She said she had had the gift since she was a child. She said it was like the movie *Poltergeist*. I was totally freaked out. All I wanted to do was leave town, so I counted the days. She tried to discuss commitment, but I was evasive. My transfer was an opportunity too important to throw away. By now, I wouldn't have stayed anyway.

The day I left, she was literally clinging to my car window. I made no promises, telling her this was it. A couple of months later, she sent me a birthday present. It was awkwardly wrapped, and the gift wasn't much better. As cruel as it seemed, I threw it away. Later that night, the phone rang. I don't know how she got my number, but it was her. Her voice was shaky. She had something important to tell me. She was pregnant.

"You're what?" I said.

She was on the pill all right, but for the wrong reasons. Something about her estrogen levels were wrong and the dosage she was taking rendered the pill ineffective for birth control. I didn't know if it was true or just a ploy to get me back. I frantically called my best friend in that town to get his opinion. He said he would check into it for me. As the months went by, and up until the time she would have supposedly delivered, he assured me that she didn't look or even act pregnant. No one in town could confirm the story, either. Not only did that event scare me away from even *attempting* to have sex for years, but also I partially blamed it for the failure of my potential medical career.

Ms. Robinson

Oh boy, here we go. We met at a party at a friend's house. It was a great bunch to be with. I met her and her best friend at the same time. I later found out that her friend liked me, also. Her friend went to excuse herself and when she returned, Ms. Robinson was giving me her number. Her friend was disappointed, but don't worry, she's the next chapter after this one. Anyway, Ms. Robinson was tall, somewhat stylish, gainfully employed, and independent. I was drawn to her looks, her mannerism, and her deep voice. She also had my favorite body type. Oh yea, did I mention that I was twenty-five and she was forty-two?

On our first date, I went to her condo and rang the bell. Her son answered. He wasn't much younger than me! He towered over me at six feet something and he was very husky.

"I'm here for your mother," I said in a timid voice.

After introductions and a quick tour of her place, we headed out.

I turned and said to her son, "I'll have her back by 11:00."

We laughed. I'm not sure I remember where we went. I think it was to a popular local Italian restaurant—one of her favorites. We had a nice evening and planned to see each other again soon. A few dates later, we somehow ended up at a planetarium in a town a couple of hours away from ours. We fooled around a little in the dark, under the "stars." That was exciting. Afterwards, we had dinner at a local restaurant. At dinner, she began to inquire about sex. She didn't understand why I hadn't made any serious advances. I assured her she was very desirable. So I explained my reluctance after the disastrous experience with The Mole. Ms. Robinson assured me she couldn't get pregnant.

The next date was at my place. I lived in another town about thirty minutes away from hers. I was pretty nervous, but she skillfully coaxed me into the bedroom.

She reassured me, and literally said, "Let me show you what women want."

That was an offer I couldn't refuse! It had been two-and-one-half years since my last (and first) experience.

She taught me things I thought I'd never do. She was very uninhibited. She had tried just about everything. I couldn't get enough of her. She had a beautiful body, with small breasts and great hips. She taught me how to enjoy things I thought I wouldn't. Most importantly, she taught me the proper "techniques" to please her. I enjoyed exploring and learning. Ironically, I now loved cunnilingus. From then on, I was hooked on this thing called sex. In a way, I loved her. In my mind, we were exclusive and committed.

However, I had no clue what was going on back in her town. Apparently, she was dating other men. Just two or three months into our relationship, she told me she had met someone else, and thought it would be best if we didn't see each other any more. I was devastated. One last "pity fuck" was in store. It was the best one of all. I think I blurted out "I love you" at the height of climax—partly because I thought I did, and partly to try to win her back. I'm sure that only scared her away for good.

After she left, I cried for her in the shower. How cruel it was for her to finally get my motor running for the first time in my life and then take away the keys. We hadn't even tried everything she liked to do. But in the long run, I owe it all to her. She did me a favor, and I have been thankful for it many times over.

Incredibly, about twelve years or so later, I was having dinner with business associates at the very same restaurant we went to on our first date. As I was leaving after dinner, I looked over and saw her. I knew it was her. Our eyes locked. She still had that classic look, although her hair was gray now. We recognized each other, but I didn't go over to meet her because she was obviously with her husband and a group of other people as well. She looked surprised, but also had a look that said "Please don't come over here!" I just smiled and kept going. It was enough to let me know she was okay and apparently settled. Good for her. Now that I'm around the age she was when we dated, I'm waiting for my twenty-five-year-old "student" to come along so I can return the favor. Yea Baby! Come to daddy!

Spare Me

About six months later, I found a way to contact Ms. Robinson's best friend, Spare Me. Anxious about getting rusty with my newfound skills, I was ready to try my luck once more. I gave her a call, and she agreed to meet for dinner. Oh well, here we go again. Although they were the same age, these two were very different physically and personality-wise. Spare Me was very petite and cute, with short, black hair and a well-proportioned body. We got along well and continued to see each other.

She told me she was disappointed when she saw Ms. Robinson giving me her number at that party where we had all met. However, she was forgiving, and we forged a relationship. We played tennis, dined out, and went to the movies. She had a long-term stable career, and drove a Carmen Ghia. She had a pleasant personality from what I remember, but nothing about her really stood out enough to make me seriously fall for her or anything. She was a fun girlfriend with an adventurous side. I once took her for a ride on my motorcycle.

Then there was the time we explored a new building under construction downtown. We were several floors up. I don't remember how many exactly, but there were no windows installed yet. We peered out over the city from this open hole in the wall, and then began to kiss. I wanted to get more adventurous with a display of exhibitionism, but I chickened out. I figured that if too many people saw us, we would get arrested for trespassing, or worse.

Inevitably, the time came for intimacy. Being the romantic I am, I decided to take her to a romantic hotel in another city for the Fourth of July. I arranged to have a dozen roses waiting for us in the suite. From our top floor balcony, we could have easily watched the fireworks. However, our plans were changed by human nature. We started fooling around and we couldn't help but become intimate.

She did something I thought was incredibly erotic for a first-time event. She took off all her clothes and laid down on the bed with her eyes closed. She just waited for me there while I undressed. She was beautifully proportioned, and I savored the moment before I ever touched her. The anticipation was all she could bear. What would I do to her? Where would I begin? She didn't open her eyes the entire time. She just wanted to *feel* the experience. I respected her implicit trust by proceeding slowly and gently. This took a lot of pressure off me. There was no expectation of performance, even though I did almost all of the performing.

Afterwards, we made it to dinner and then went downtown for a close-up view of the fireworks. It was a wonderful evening, with elements of adventure and romance. We continued to date for about six months, as I recall. I began to realize there wasn't an emotional bond. Our relationship revolved around one thing, and I wanted to move on. She was intimately very passive, compared to Ms. Robinson, who was very aggressive.

Although my intentions were good, actually I was still emotionally immature. I wasn't able to meet her needs other than physical, and I really didn't know what to do beyond that. So I planned a meeting to tell her. I brought a gift for her, but it bombed. It was a mug with funny phrases on it (she drank coffee). I thought it would cheer her up, but she seemed to take it kind of hard. I think I actually did her a favor. I thought about them both for many years afterwards.

Midnight

We were set up by a mutual business acquaintance. The acquaintance gave me Midnight's business card. We talked over the phone a couple of times and then set up a lunch date. We met at a local restaurant. It was July 29. I was pleasantly surprised when she walked in. She was good-looking and very sexy. She was the "Daisy Duke" type. There was not an ounce of fat on her. Her auburn hair was long and thick, and those teeth—white as snow, even though she smoked. She was from the northeast, and was a few years younger than me.

She was not the least bit pretentious. She was down to earth, as if she didn't realize she was so good looking. Needless to say, lunch was a hit. She told me she thought I was good looking, too. Those two words and my name had never been spoken in the same sentence. Had I finally emerged from my nerd cocoon as a budding cool guy? I had always wanted to be a cool guy with a cool girl, and this was my best shot so far.

We planned for dinner the next night. I picked her up at her place out in the country. It was sparsely furnished, with nothing more than she really needed. We went out and things went well. There were no real romantic sparks, but a definite attraction. I remember all of her particulars. She liked cold French fries. Her favorite color was red. Her favorite car was a corvette, and her favorite band was Bob Seger.

On this date, I decided to try something different—a sort of "make up for lost time" theme. Back at her place, I decided to get aggressive. She resisted somewhat, but didn't really fight me off, either. We fooled around on the back of her Taurus; no, not in the back seat; on the trunk. The small spoiler was just enough to keep her hips in the right place. She cooled things down before I got very far, but we agreed to another date.

Soon came the next dinner date. We began to discover that we had very different backgrounds. She was nice, but not overly personable. Still, I wanted to pursue the relationship. She was so different from anyone I had ever dated before, and I was excited about developing a relationship with her. Back at her place, again things progressed. I continued with my new strategy, and it worked. She gave in. Whether it was because she really wanted to, or because she just wanted to get rid of me, it didn't matter at the time. It was late; very late.

She was unbelievable. She had the perfect Playboy body—every inch. Even her feet were perfect. Never had I experienced anything like it before. It was the best sex I had ever had or even fantasized about. She probably doesn't even remember it. She was quite acrobatic. We were on the couch, and it was literally bouncing across the wooden living room floor. The dog was barking, and the cat ran away.

I was so overwhelmed that I broke down in tears afterwards. So much for "Mr. Tuff Guy." I had been going through a long, difficult, and unhappy period in my life.

"Please tell me you weren't faking it," I said. "I can't take anymore lies."

Then she said something I've never forgotten, "I'm soaking wet! I can't fake that."

I blew the speakers in my car on the way home. I called one of my best friends when I got home. He woke up agitated, but to this day he says he's never heard me more ecstatic before. I've known him for thirty years.

I tried to continue the relationship after that, but things changed. She needed a few things, so I did what I could for her. She could have drained me financially. If I could, I would have given her everything I had (except someone else had beaten her to it). After awhile, she wouldn't return my calls. When I did get a hold of her, she was always "busy" or "had other plans." We never went out again. I've always wondered why. Actually, we were mismatched, but I would have gladly been her boyfriend. I suspected that she had recently broken up with someone and I was the revenge date.

On the way home from one of our dates, we stopped by a local grocery store to get her child a book bag. School started the next week. There were only two or three left on the rack. They were the ones no one else wanted. One was on the floor and looked like it had been stepped on a few times. It was late, and no other stores were open. It was sad. Her child started school without a book bag, but she told me she managed to get him one later that week.

She was so selfless. She sacrificed greatly for her kid. I've heard about it before, but I've never witnessed a woman going without food to support her child. That trait about her captured my interest. She was such a totally selfless person, despite a rough childhood. I admired her for that, but felt sorry for her at the same time. Things weren't easy for her. In the end, she helped me more than she knew. With renewed confidence (i.e. ego), I set a course for uncharted women from then on.

Years later, I dropped in on her out of the blue. It was near Christmas. "The ghost of Christmas past," I said, when I saw her. She still had it. She looked great and had kept in shape. We caught up on the past years. She was cordial. She showed me a picture of her kid. He was so big, I didn't recognize him. As we hugged goodbye, I told her if there was anything I could do for her, just to let me know. Still, we had no date. I gave her my card, anyway. I wished her well. Her cat never did come back.

Yoga Bitch

At this point, I was a member of an incredible singles club, which held fabulous monthly parties. Hundreds of people would show up, the bands were great, and it was all over the Internet. It was at one of those parties when there was this lady who caught every man's attention because of what she was wearing. Or should I say what she wasn't wearing. She was thin and pretty with shoulder-length curly blonde hair. She was wearing a black skirt and a sheer black blouse. It was so sheer that it looked like it wasn't even there. It was completely see-through, like something from Fredrick's of Hollywood. Oh yea, she was wearing a black bra. She had an attractive and slender figure. All the guys, including me, were just staring at her. Many of them went up to introduce themselves, but it was hard to concentrate on a conversation with a woman basically in her underwear. Okay ladies, let me clarify something for you: When you blatantly advertise the goods, men think you're either easy or for sale. Eventually, my turn came around, and I tried hard to look her in the face. She made a comment about why the other men kept staring at her name tag and I wasn't.

I said, "Honey, it's not your name tag they're looking at."

She laughed and thought her blouse wasn't a big deal. I agreed and we conversed long enough for me to ask her out. It turned out she was a psychologist and she was very interesting.

The weekend came and I went to her house. It was a small, older house that was not well maintained. The front yard was covered with lots of branches and twigs everywhere. I walked up and rang the doorbell. I think it didn't work, so I had to knock. She answered and invited me in. Thank goodness she was wearing something conservative. Her house was sparsely furnished without much decoration. She didn't own a TV. I made a comment about her yard needing some work. She asked if I was volunteering to clean it for her, and that ended that conversation.

We set out for dinner. She wanted to go to a favorite restaurant of hers and I wanted to try a new place that had opened recently. So we compromised and ate dinner at one restaurant, and then went for dessert and drinks at the other. She was interesting, but distanced herself somewhat. She was the earthy, vegetarian type. She stated she might be moving to Oregon or Washington or somewhere on the west coast. She sat in the chair with her legs crossed, Indian style. Later, she got up and stared out of the window for awhile. That's not a very encouraging sign during a date. She seemed kind of funky, but I still found her attractive. I think I really just wanted to see if she had more of those sheer blouses, or maybe matching skirts!

Then I got a stomachache and had to be excused for awhile. How romantic. We didn't exactly click, and soon it was time to take her home. When we got there, I was ready to leave. Surprisingly, she invited me back in and fixed me some green tea. She didn't have any regular tea, or soda, or anything else. After a short conversation, she said "Excuse me, but I have to do my yoga now." She did it every night and didn't want to miss this one, even though I was there. So instead of just asking me to leave, she simply excused herself and came back from the bedroom wearing only leotards. Then she laid down on the wooden floor facing me and started contorting like a snake shedding its skin.

I sipped my green tea and thought what in the world my next move should be. After awhile, I began to squirm as I tried not to get excited watching her. Then without skipping a beat, she laid on her back facing me, with her legs spread apart and started raising her hips up and down off the floor. Okay, that did it. All I could see was her crotch in detail.

So I finally said, "How much longer are you going to do this?"

She asked why, and I told her I was uncomfortable watching her.

She said, "Oh, you men are all alike! Is sex all you ever think about?"

I said "No, but it's hard to avoid the thought while you're lying directly in front of me doing pelvic thrusts."

Then one of us decided it might be best if I just left. She saw me to the door, and I paused and turned to her. She gave me a hug and said goodnight. I asked for a kiss, and she rolled her eyes and said something like "Oh, good grief." She gave me a quick peck and shut the door quicker than a cuckoo clock.

I stood there puzzled for a moment, like the Grinch did on Christmas morning when the *Whos* came out to sing. I pondered over the see-through blouse, the leotards, and pelvic thrusts. All that teasing for nothing, I wondered, as I stumbled over the twigs walking back to my car in the dark. I'm not real sure, but I think we actually had a second date. Or maybe that was the second date. I can't remember. Maybe I am a typical guy after all. I'm not sure if we went out once or twice, but I could certainly describe her body to you!

SEX FOR THE BRAIN

Back at another singles' club party, I glanced over and saw this incredibly cute lady timidly smiling at me. Then she looked away and took a sip of her drink, trying not to smile. When she looked back, I was already on my way over. She couldn't help but crack a grin; she knew I was coming straight for her. We introduced ourselves and immediately hit it off. We were almost instantly infatuated with each other. She was cute, petite, and spoke with a northern accent. She was a good ten or eleven years older than I was, but she didn't look her age at all. I made her show me her driver's license to prove it. We left the main room to seek a quieter place in the hotel to talk, without having to yell over the band. We were together the rest of the night. We giggled like school kids. She was very intellectual, and that really turned me on. It turned out that she was another psychologist, but she didn't know Yoga Bitch. As the evening ended, I boldly kissed her goodbye.

Although I lived some distance away, it was drivable and we agreed to see each other again soon. We saw each other about twice a week for several months. Most of the time, she would meet me in a city about halfway between us. Sometimes I would "drop in" on her and surprise her at her practice. We had the most intellectual conversations about everything from politics to relationships. We discussed at length our previous relationships and helped each other to understand them better. We would go shopping together, and I didn't mind. I actually spent three hours one time in an Ann Taylor store watching her try on clothing. She introduced me to a great group of friends. We made out and fooled around like kids. She relished my infamous quote, "I'll never get married again, no matter how good the blow-jobs are!"

One time, we met at a movie theater to see a show, but we never made it into the theater. We got too "distracted" with each other in the car, right there in the parking lot. Another time, we met at a Barnes and Noble, and we almost didn't make it inside there, either. So why couldn't we just go to her house and get it over with, you ask? Well, she was in a very unusual situation. She and her husband were "permanently separated," but still lived in the same house with separate bedrooms. It was sort of a co-habitation of convenience until the house sold. So they planned their weekends very carefully around their social life.

She had a wonderful home in a nice neighborhood. She had a beautiful teenaged daughter, and an elusive cat that would come back to haunt me in the near future. One night I stayed over because I was doing business in town the next day. Her ex was there. I slept on the sofa bed downstairs in the den. It was kind of strange, with all three of us in the same house. Anyway, just as I was about to fall asleep, curiosity killed the cat. It jumped on me in the dark, and then hung around to check me out. Evidently it liked me, because it settled down right on my ass and began to clean itself. Soon it hiked up one leg and began licking its ass the way cats do, but it was also inadvertently licking mine, too. I didn't find this kinky at all. This was not the kind of pussy I had been hoping for. I rolled over and sent that cat on its way. I didn't sleep well the rest of the night. The next morning we got up and had breakfast in the kitchen with her ex-husband—her gay ex-husband. It was a Twilight Zone moment.

Then one day came the "opportunity." The house would be available all afternoon; no kids, and no ex-gay husband-father whatever-the-hell-he-was. It was our best and only chance up to that point. So the big day had finally arrived. She had condoms, but they weren't the right kind. (Just never mind.) We had to go to the store to buy some more. We got back with eager anticipation. It was a hot sunny afternoon. The yardman was there working in the front yard. Alone at last, upstairs we went, hopped in the bed, and off came the clothes.

As we began to fool around, a sudden thump startled us. This bird had flown into the bedroom's glass window. Shaken, but not stirred, it recovered and for some reason tried again. For the next half hour, this damned bird kept flying from a branch in the front yard straight into the glass every few minutes. This obviously broke our concentration as we tried to proceed. About that time, for some reason, the yardman rang the doorbell. We ignored it. He rang again and again. We still ignored him. The postman only rings twice, but this yard guy just didn't get it. Well, then it turns out the house wasn't *completely* empty after all. Now here came the cat, curious as always. It hopped up into the bed, and Sex for the Brain had to get up and take it back out of the room and close the door. Well, the cat didn't like this, so it began to scratch and meow at the door, on top of everything else. Now I don't know about you, but I couldn't make love in broad daylight with a kamikaze bird banging into the window, a yardman ringing the doorbell, and a separation-anxiety-ridden cat hollering at the bedroom door.

It was such a disaster; we couldn't get around to doing very much. In short, "it" didn't happen. So we decided to escape to the shower in the bathroom. It was plenty big enough for two people, but more disaster awaited us. The water came out like a fire hydrant and splashed us so forcefully it actually hurt. It just wasn't meant for us to succeed that day. It was just as well. We turned out to be great friends, and analyzed our dating life and relationships with others. I know I cried on her shoulder at least once over periods of personal crisis. I've kept in loose touch with her over the years.

LEAVE A MESSAGE

I had gone out of town one day just to eat at my favorite restaurant, to shop, and to catch a show. It was only about an hour away. After the movie, as I drove out of the parking lot, my cell phone indicated that I had a message. It was a woman who said a mutual friend told her to give me a call and introduce herself. She left her name and number, and said she would like to meet. Now that's a message you don't get every day. Ego soaring, I turned on the radio, and one of my favorite songs came on just then. What an unexpected fun day that was. It was July 29—one year to the day since I had met Midnight.

I called her when I got home. She seemed pleasant and upbeat. We agreed to meet at a favorite local restaurant in town. She was medium height, slender, with short curly red hair and piercing blue eyes. (Okay, maybe they were green; it's been a few years.) She had an optimistic outlook on life but was practical at the same time. Her smile was infectious. She was stably employed and her children were grown for the most part. The night was pleasant, and we agreed to meet again. I kissed her goodbye in the parking lot. It was short, but what a great kiss. It was right up there with the best of them. Isn't it amazing how such a simple act can be so different from one person to the next?

We met for lunch the next week. I picked her up from work and we ate nearby. She shared with me some personal tragedies she had been through. I told her she seemed to have overcome her challenges well. She was also contemplating a career change. She had reached her advancement potential and was getting bored with her work. Her new career would take her out of state. I shared with her that I was at a difficult stage in my life and things were unstable due to circumstances beyond my control—divorce. We pretty much

51

determined that only friendship was in order for us. Damn, I wanted another one of those incredible kisses.

She invited me to a group meeting she regularly attended. It was sort of an informal religion-based, self-help group for divorcees. So I started attending one evening each week. At first, it was just because of her. Then it turned out that this was a crucial group for me as my circumstances grew worse over time. A couple of months later, her career opportunity came and she moved to another state. I kept going to the meetings for over a year. They were good friends who helped me through the lowest point in my life. The last I heard about her was that she had met someone and was very happy. Someday, it would be my turn.

Z3

On the news, they said that it was the coldest December in 100 years. It was late in the evening. No customers were around. Then here she came; her car limping into the dealership lot with a flat tire. Like dogs in heat, all the guys ran out to rescue her. However, I had a better plan. It was one of the smoothest plans I had ever devised, especially on the spur of the moment. I knew it would take awhile for them to change the tire, and it was awfully cold out there. I figured she would come inside and wait. So I meandered over to the coffee pot and poured two cups. Then I waited on the leather couch by the warm fireplace. Sure enough, she came in only a moment later.

She was incredible. Not cute, not pretty, just damn good looking as hell. She had long blonde hair with wavy curls. It was sort of like a Farrah Fawcett style, but not as dramatic. I think she had green eyes. She couldn't have weighed more than 105 pounds. My ego swelled as she approached. (I was too nervous for anything else to be swelling). I offered her a cup of coffee, which she accepted. We talked for awhile on the couch by the fire. No lines or lies on my part, just a fascination with this person who had just walked into my life. We got to know a little about each other, as the guys took longer than expected outside. (Try finding the spare tire on a Z3 in the dark.) Stretching my fledgling sales skills, I tried to interest her in a second vehicle. For some reason, we must have been out of brochures for the model she wanted. So I volunteered to bring some to her workplace when we got them.

A few days later, I took some to her, and that's when I asked her out to dinner. I was speechless when she accepted. How does a woman like this not have a boyfriend? She gave me her number and we planned to have dinner a few days later. She worked in town but lived in another about an hour away. My car was in the shop when the day came, so I borrowed a loaner—a used loaner; *very* used. So I made the trek. I believe we met in a Wal-Mart parking lot and then I followed her to her place. It was clean and tidy. The kids were at their father's house that weekend. She showed me their pictures. Her children were beautiful. They looked like angels. I didn't tell her that, though. For dinner, we took her car. She had replaced the bad tire by now. It was a polite date, as I recall—nothing outstanding, but not a disaster, either. We had a nice time and agreed to another meeting. Back at her place, we talked some more and watched part of "Urban Cowboy" on TV. Then came the goodnight kiss. It was great. After we finished, I walked to the door, stopped, and then turned back. She was standing in the same spot. She hadn't moved.

She was so good looking I couldn't resist going back for more. In a *Body Heat* moment, I closed the door, marched back to her, grabbed her in my arms, and kissed her ever so passionately again. She didn't resist. I was still grinning from ear to ear as I hit the highway. Like the Christmas song, I figured "All the way home I'll be warm." That is, until the engine light came on. It was late, and the temperature was maybe in the teens, at best. Most of the trip was downhill, so I coasted a lot. I luckily made it back without any trouble.

We met for lunch downtown the next week. When we walked in, everyone looked at us. The women hated her, and the men hated me. It was delicious. After that, my ego was soaring much higher than my bank account. There was good news: she was buying a house and moving to town. The bad news, as I found out later, was that I wasn't going to be a part of it. Valentine's Day was approaching, so I tried one last time to win her over. I went to her workplace and delivered her a gift along with a letter. I wish I had saved that one to have for this book. She just wasn't the romantic type, I guess. She probably liked the football quarterback type of guy. I was more like the punter, and it was fourth down. So I got punted.

Psycho

Yes, there's one in every crowd. This time it was my turn to meet one. A co-worker set us up. She told Psycho to call me one day at work, and we set a date for that night. It happened to be July 29 for the third consecutive year. She happened to have some shade of red hair just like the others. (On that date the following year, I was dating Beacon, whose hair was as bright red as the sun.) I picked her up at her house. It was clean and cozy. We went to a nice restaurant for dinner. It was soon apparent to me that we weren't going to be a match, but after a chocolate martini, she was having a blast. She was loud and obnoxious, and carried a few extra pounds. I tried to keep the conversation light, but I couldn't loosen up as much as she had. She began to laugh loudly at whatever I said, and shouted "Woo-Hoo." Red flags went up. I remember just wanting to get her back in the car and away from public. Her personality began to swing widely from aggressive to passive. She was nice one moment, and then without warning, she would get angry at something for no reason.

Back home, she invited me in. She showed me lots of pictures of her worldly travels. She spread them out on her bed, so we were lying in bed looking at the pictures. I was uncomfortable with this, so when we finished looking, I made my way back out to the couch in the living room. All the while I was beginning to get a little afraid of her because she was behaving so unpredictably. She would laugh out loud one minute and be sad or angry the next. The red flags had now changed to signal flairs—the kind sinking ships use when calling, "May-Day!" She gave me a glass of wine or something, and I mistakenly accepted it. She sat down next to me and began to get aggressive. The next thing I knew, we were making out and her hands were wandering over my body. After a little bit of this, she got up and went to the bathroom. She was in there for a very long time.

I got nervous again, and began to wonder what she was doing. Then paranoia began to set in. I wondered if she was harming herself, or if she would come out with a gun or something and try to harm me. I was shocked when she came out about fifteen minutes later, completely naked. I guess she was trying to insert a diaphragm or something. For some reason, naked women don't look very threatening, especially after a glass of wine. The signal flairs faded as the blood drained from my head and flowed into other areas.

She threw herself at me and I figured, "What the hell? She's drunk and I'll never see her again, so why not go for it?" Maybe I'm just too uptight, and a good sexual release is what I needed. So, back into the bedroom we went.

She was loud and aggressive. We wrestled around, sort of like rugby players. I thought the neighbors certainly must have heard us. When we finished, she hopped up and went back to the bathroom to "clean up." I immediately regretted what had just happened. She came back out while I was getting dressed. She said next time she would cook dinner for me to return the favor of buying dinner for her. I said okay and left shortly thereafter, with no intention of seeing her again.

She began calling me at work and bugging me about the next date. I tried to put her off, saying I was busy, but she would get upset. So I reluctantly agreed to let her fix me dinner at her place. I went, knowing I would have to explain to her that things weren't going to work out. She made me a nice dinner and we talked afterwards out on the patio. Again, she displayed unstable behavior. No alcohol for me, this time. I kept my distance and nervously told her that there was no chemistry between us. She wasn't too happy about that, and was pressing me for an explanation. Of course, I couldn't say, "You're psycho," so I danced around the subject and stated that our interests were different, and there was just no chemistry. One minute I got a lecture about how all I wanted was to use her for sex, and the next minute, she would plead with me, stating how good it was. I was really afraid of her now. She would say things that didn't make any sense and then just laugh like a maniac about it. I just wanted to get out of there with my life. The movie, *Fatal Attraction* came to mind. I kept being nice and slowly made my way to the door. She made statements something like, "You'll regret it," or, "You'll miss me," etc. We parted when she was in one of her "friendly" moods. What a relief it was just to leave in one piece.

Back at work, her friend asked me how things were going. I had to tell her that it wasn't going to work out. I tried to jokingly play it off by saying, "Oh, she's too wild for me." Well, I should have known by then that women talk. So, the next day or so, I got a call at work. Psycho was angry and yelling at me for "slandering" her in that way. I just hung up on her and told the receptionist not to take anymore of her calls. I looked for booby traps under my car for the next few days. That's what you get for thinking with the wrong head. Luckily, I never did hear back from her. Maybe she got a hold of some other poor shmuck. Maybe she threw herself in front of a train. Maybe Yoga Bitch could counsel her. I don't know and I don't want to know.

Fly Me

My dear friend, Annette, set up this date. She knew me well, and knew I would like her friend. So we all decided to meet one night at a restaurant. It was Annette and her fiancé, myself and Fly Me. I got there early, and took a good look around. I had only a description, plus she was about ten years older than me. I didn't see her, so I waited in the foyer area of the restaurant beside a lighted fake palm tree. After about ten minutes or so, a beautiful lady walked up to me from inside the restaurant, and asked me if I was the one she was waiting for. I was surprised. She didn't look anything like her age, and I had completely overlooked her earlier.

She was a former stewardess for a major airline who was changing careers. She was short and petite with shoulder-length blonde hair, a beautiful figure, and a beautiful face. Her eyes were bright and sparkling, and her lips were full and perfectly shaped. Annette had hit a home run as far as I was concerned. Soon afterwards, Annette and her fiancé arrived and we were all seated for dinner. After the usual small talk, I tried to get a feel for her opinion of me. She was polite, but a little hard to read. She ordered just a salad, which offended me a little. I thought that she was trying to save me money or something, as if I couldn't afford to buy her dinner. Later, I was assured she was just a light eater.

Dinner was a hit, and afterwards we went to a karaoke bar. I was smart enough not to get up and sing, but I think we danced during one number. It was a good evening. When it was time to leave, I still didn't have a reassuring feeling from her. Annette said that she liked me, so I asked her if I could call her. She gave me her number. A few days later, I followed up.

We met for lunch a week or so later (same old story, she lived an hour and a half away). I knew my luck with long-distance relationships was usually bad, but these women were so gorgeous, I just had to try. While driving down an unfamiliar road, I unknowingly got caught going through a red light by one of those photo-enforced intersections. I was looking for a street sign and didn't see the light change. I got my picture ticket in the mail a couple of weeks later. I would have preferred to be pulled over the old fashioned way, by a real officer. At least, maybe I could have pleaded my case, "But officer, I've got a date with a hot blonde stewardess! What stoplight?" Anyway, we met at an old former favorite restaurant of mine. I think she ate real food this time. Again, she was polite and friendly, but a little distant.

She was excited about starting her new career in massage therapy. She was so pretty and I was becoming a little infatuated with her. However, at the same time, I had a feeling that 100 other men were after her. When lunch was finished, she asked me how much she owed for her portion.

I looked at the tab and said, "It says here you owe me a hug."

She smiled and thanked me. I walked her out to the car. My intuition told me to go for it because I may never get to see her again.

We hugged goodbye beside her car, and then I held her by the shoulders with my hands and said, "I've just got to kiss you!"

She said okay, and we broke the rule on not displaying public affection. The wind was blowing hard and her hair was in the way a little. It was another one of those, "Oh my God" kisses. What an impact she made with her lips! They were every bit as good as they looked. It was powerful and soft at the same time. It truly was one of the best kisses of my life, and I guess I've had a few to go by. As she got into her car, I stood there for a moment, trying not to look dumbfounded. I didn't even care that I was standing by a four-lane highway with my pants bulging. Sometimes this assertive stuff works out all right! I was glad I did it, because she wouldn't return my calls after that day. My mouth got the only massage I was going to get from her. I envy the lucky guy who's getting the personal massage therapy now.

Part III:
One-Date Wonders

Here's where things get interesting. We've all been there. Most of you will be able to identify with some of these stories. From wonderful to disastrous, I think I've had some unique dates, to say the least. The scary part is there will be more to come. Some of you were unforgettable. Some were just dates. Some were at least a good story. Still others were uneventful and left out altogether. Isn't it funny how some were unforgettable for me, but to them I was probably forgettable.

I think most readers will find this section useful, whether or not you are single. For those readers who are married, this section should be enough to keep you married. For those readers who are single, you may find comfort in this section knowing that you are not alone in your experiences.

Strangers in the Rye

This was more of an experience than a date—a taste of dating life to come. I don't know what the heck I was doing in that particular city at the time, but that's not the point. Maybe I was at a wedding or something; I don't remember. It was many years ago. I went into a nice restaurant in one of the better parts of town for dinner. I guess I stood out by sitting alone. Two women were sitting at an adjacent table, and they kept checking me out. I had this strange feeling I was about to be picked up. I guess I wasn't in the mood for games that evening, because I distinctly remember trying to avert the inevitable. I was wearing a ring with a stone in it on my right hand. I took the ring off and put it on my left hand, and then turned the stone inward so it would look like a wedding band from the outside. I really don't remember why I made such an effort to avoid them, but my effort failed. One of them invited me to join them for dinner. I said I was fine, thank you. But she persisted until she wore me down. It was more embarrassing to have her talking to me from across two tables.

So I joined them. I don't remember any names or much else about the conversation. The one who asked me to join them did all the talking, and the next thing I knew, the other lady was gone. I didn't see her for the rest of the night. Dinner and a few glasses of wine later, this lady began to get suggestive, and then aggressive with me. During the conversation, we discovered our mutually favorite TV show was Dallas. It must have been a Friday night, because she invited me back to her place to watch it with her—on her bed. I was terrified. Keep in mind I was about twenty, and still unsure of myself.

I said something stupid like I didn't want to "miss" the show. Then she tried to persuade me a little more. The next thing I knew, we were making out heavily. She sort of attacked me. This wasn't the type of restaurant where things like this were appropriate. Throwing caution to the wind, the tablecloth somehow got tangled up in our escapade. I remember hearing utensils hitting the floor and glassware overturning. We were the center of attention (little did I know that many years later this scenario would repeat itself, but that's another chapter). Amazingly, we weren't asked to leave. Even more amazing, I found some kind of excuse to leave without her. I would watch Dallas alone that night, and I still missed the plot.

Having second thoughts about the night before, I called her the next morning. With renewed confidence (and a little regret), I told her I wanted to see her again and tried to invite myself over to her place. She told me I wasn't ready for this. I told her I was now! (As if I had turned into James Bond overnight or something.) I guess turning down her one-night-stand offer offended her. How would I explain to the guys that I had turned down a woman who threw herself at me? So I did what most college guys would do. I turned the story around and told them she turned down *my* advances. Yea, she didn't know what she was missing. A few pats on the back and "better luck next time" assurances restored my ego. My virtue was safe once again.

Going Down?

Some of my best friends and I were in one of our favorite bars. It was located in a grand old hotel in a resort town. We frequented this place to listen to good music and enjoy an eclectic mix of patrons of all ages. The four of us were seated at a table somewhere in the middle of the room. On this night, there was a particularly attractive woman sitting at the bar. She had long blondish-brown hair with an exotic, high-class type of appeal. We began to discuss her, and as guys do, dared each other to make the first move. I and another guy liked her more than the others, so it came down to one of us. He decided to buy her a drink. He told the waitress to send her another one of whatever it was she was having. We all waited with anticipation to see her response.

Soon after her free drink, she came over to our table to thank him, but she thanked *me* instead. The other guy quickly spoke up and told her that he was the one who sent her the drink. She thanked him, but then sat down next to me. To our surprise, she basically ignored him and struck up a conversation with the other three of us. We tried not to laugh out loud at the situation. It turned out she was some sort of cosmetic salesperson from out of town. I can't remember exactly, but I think she was either part French, or from France, because she had an exotic French-sounding last name. She was several years older than us—a whopping twenty-five years old. Can you remember when you aspired to be twenty-five? We must have been about twenty or twenty-one. She had incredibly smooth skin and was strikingly attractive. She was staying at the hotel for the night. She seemed interested in me for some reason, and I was incredibly intimidated by her. She was sort of aggressive, placing her hand on my thigh, for example. I didn't know what to do. Thank goodness my buddies were there to fill in the gaps.

After awhile, we decided to go to another nearby bar. She decided to follow us. The guy who bought her the drink didn't come with us. After all, he had pretty much been shot down by her. So we went to this other nice bar and continued our conversations for a few hours longer. Then it came time for her to go back to the hotel. It wasn't really late, but she said she had to leave in the morning and wanted to get back. Soon, I discovered that wasn't the reason she wanted to get back at all. Unbeknownst to me, she had other plans.

I followed her out to her car to say goodnight. She asked me to come back to the hotel with her. Scared to death, I said I couldn't do that. She said she'd make it worth my while. I came up with the excuse that my buddies were drunk and I had to drive them home. She then asked for a kiss goodnight, so I leaned in through her car window. As we kissed, she grabbed my hand and shoved it right up her skirt while spreading her legs! This nearly put me into cardiac arrest. I said I really had to go check on my buddies. She asked me if I would at least join her for breakfast the next day before she left. I said okay, and went back into the bar. Like all guys that age do (but would never admit it), I sniffed my fingers. It was my first real whiff of "it." I was astonished and amazed. My fingers had almost lost their virginity. Way to go, guys! I didn't wash my hand for two days. I excitedly told my friends about the event, and they told me what an idiot I was for not going back with her. They tried to encourage me to go, but I was so intimidated by her that I probably wouldn't have been able to perform.

She must have sensed that I was clueless and was probably only interested in me for that reason—some female version of superiority conquest, I imagine. She certainly could have had any other man she wanted, but I was the sacrificial virgin, literally. She seemed "experienced" and aggressive. I would have fumbled with the basics. I wanted to avoid that humiliation.

So the next morning came and I called to see if she was still interested. She said yes, so off I went to the hotel. She met me in the lobby and asked if I wanted to come up and see the room. I said sure, so we went to her room. It was nice, and she was about half-packed. Nothing aggressive happened, thank goodness. I guess she had given up on me. So we went back down the elevator to the main level. When the doors opened, there stood my hometown mayor and a state senator, both of whom were good friends with my family. I turned about three shades of red. They were equally surprised. We introduced ourselves and then they announced that they were about to have breakfast also, and naturally they asked us to join them. We declined, but ended up sitting at the table beside them anyway. I think one of them was quite proud of me. You know, the old, "I didn't know you had it in you" attitude. After breakfast, she went back to her room alone to finish packing. There were no more kisses or anything, just goodbye this time. I tried to get her number to call for a future date, but she said she traveled a lot and would be hard to reach. How ironic, because about eight hours earlier, she was not only within my reach, but she was literally in my grasp! A hard lesson learned.

I'm sure my family heard all about it before I ever got back home. However, they never said anything to me about it. Thank goodness I didn't have to explain to my father what I was doing coming down the elevator from a hotel room with an older, exotic French woman. How could I? No one would have believed me, anyway.

Looking back on this and the previous chapter, it's hard to believe that women intimidated me so much back then. Nowadays, I realize that life is too short for such foolish things. The only women who intimidate me now are the ones who have been married for twenty or thirty years. How do they do it? I can only imagine.

Goofy

My best friend and I were in Atlanta for a debutant ball. That week was almost unbelievable, but that story is for another book. I had been fixed up with a blind date while my friend was at the ball (I wasn't quite the escort type). Well, I heard that my date wasn't quite the debutant type, either. Eager to make the most of it and knowing I'd probably never see this chick again; I decided to play a bold joke. Before the date, I went and gathered flowers, a card, and a small box of candy. The card was the type that was blank on the inside, so you could write your own saying.

So, over we went to her house in Buckhead. She answered the door, and I immediately knew it was going to be a long night. She was pale and skinny, with large eyes and protruding ears. Worse yet, her nose turned upright, so much that I could see straight up her nostrils. She looked like the Disney cartoon character, Goofy, so that became her nickname between my friend and I.

I proceeded with my plan and first gave her the flowers.

"Oh, thank you," she said.

Then came the candy. "Oh, you're so sweet," she said.

Then I reached in my blazer pocket and pulled out the card.

"Gee, you went all out, didn't you?" she said.

"I guess so," I replied.

Then she opened the card and it read, "Okay, I've been polite. Now off with your clothes, bitch!"

The look on her face was priceless; kind of like when Goofy had stuck his finger in a light socket.

Then she shocked me by saying, "I'm going to show this to my mother!"

Thinking quick on my feet, I replied, "That's fine. I'd probably like her better than you, anyway."

"Now you two get along," said my friend.

Stuck with each other, we proceeded to her car and she was going to take me out on the town. My friend left for the Piedmont Driving Club for his evening event. We had dinner and mostly talked about our friend's relationship. She pressed me for his intentions, which I knew weren't serious. Protective of my best friend, I divulged little by playing dumb.

Later on, we were cruising down Peachtree Street in the right-hand lane, when we approached a stopped bus ahead of us.

"Oh, they'll move out of the way," she said as she pushed in the clutch and put it in neutral.

No brakes; we just coasted, waiting for that bus to pull ahead. Well, it never did, and she never hit the brakes. I braced myself for the worst with my hands on the dash (no airbags back then). So we just bumped right into the back of that bus. Then she cursed at the bus, like it was his fault.

The remainder of the night was spent driving around in endless boredom waiting for the ball to end, so we could see our friends again. I don't even remember how the night ended, so I assume it was pretty forgetful. Too bad, after such a memorable start. Oh well, maybe she eventually married a plastic surgeon.

Thunder Storm

Freedom at last! My divorce had just been finalized and one of my best friends and I were celebrating over lunch at one of our favorite restaurants. I proudly proclaimed that I was going to ask out the first woman I saw—not because I was desperate or anything, but just to celebrate the fact that now I could. About that time our waitress came over. After taking our order, I did as I had pledged and I asked her out. She accepted, and wrote her number on a napkin for me.

She had medium-length blonde hair (that day) and was average looking—not great, but not bad, either. She was maybe a few extra pounds above average, and a little rough around the edges. Hell, it didn't matter to me if she even had a penis. I was determined to conquer the single life again. So I called and we made arrangements for a date that weekend.

I went to pick her up at her house. It was modest at best. The designated parking area was the front yard. Her kids were gawking from the front door. She came out and eagerly hopped in before I could get the door for her. This didn't seem to matter or even occur to her. She was drinking a beer. After asking her where she would like to go, she said she would like to go to the restaurant where she worked. Why she wanted to go there, I'll never know. After repeated questioning, she assured me that was where she wanted to go. Something told me I should begin praying that we wouldn't run into anyone I knew there. It wasn't far from her house. On the way, she began to explain to me that she didn't have a car and she walked to work. She also informed me she had made an appointment to get her hair cut the next day and asked me if I could give her a ride. I said okay, as the red flags began going up in my head.

We soon arrived at the restaurant. We were seated out on the patio, as it was still light. She ordered an appetizer and a bottle of wine. I began to get a little nervous. I had eighty dollars in cash in my pocket and no credit cards. (I had cut them up during the divorce.) Dinner here was expensive and we hadn't even started yet. She stated for the first of many times that night that I must think she was the "town lush," but she assured me she hadn't been out in a long time and she was only having a good time (on me, of course). I guess she was smart enough to know that we weren't each other's type and she was going to make the most of it. As we ordered dinner, I got a sinking feeling in my stomach, because whatever she ordered had put me over my financial limit. Then it began to rain. So we were moved inside.

The wine had been flowing for awhile now, and she began to express her opinion of me. She kept telling me things like, "Loosen up," "Take off that tie," and "Don't be so stuffy." The wine bottle ran empty before dinner, so she ordered other drinks. As she began to knock over glasses and drop utensils on the floor during dinner, she kept assuring me she was not the "town lush." Then she decided to kiss me while she was still coordinated enough to do so. She grabbed me like a football player and began slobbering all over me. It was like the old cartoon about Pepe Le Pew, the skunk that tried to charm Sylvester the cat while he tried to squirm away. Shortly after that, management came out and informed her that she was cut off from alcohol. What a great impression to make on your co-workers.

Then she decided she needed to use the restroom. She informed me that although she knew where it was, she would need my help getting there. So off we went to the restroom. Believe me, there's no way to gracefully carry a drunk to the bathroom in a nice restaurant. Nevertheless, the journey didn't end there. I had to physically take her into the bathroom and aim her toward a stall. Red-faced, I waited outside the door until she was ready. Then we swaggered back to our table.

Now she was "refreshed" and ready for dessert and coffee. I knew I would be washing dishes to work off the tab. I braced myself as the waitress approached with that little white ticket. The bill came to $129.00.

Now what? Should I call a friend? Write an IOU? Make a dash for the door? Then she came up with a brilliant idea.

"What about the employee discount?" she asked.

"Oh yes, of course," the waitress said. "I'll be right back."

Someone above was looking out for me that night, because the "adjusted" bill came to $79.00 even. I had to ask her if she could leave the tip. She cursed about it and finally left her tip money from working lunch that day. The only thing on my mind was to get the hell out of there and never come back; but she had other plans for the night.

After we left the restaurant, she had to make me take her to the most run-down convenience store in town. It looked like a good place to get killed, especially the way I was dressed. I nervously waited in the car while she swaggered in for some cigarettes. We managed to get out of there unscathed. Finally back at her house, I was so disgusted that I was ready to kick her out on the front lawn. Then she decided to tell me about how her daddy had paid for her breast reduction surgery and was eager to show me the results. Before I knew what was going on, she had pulled her blouse up to her chin, while proudly proclaiming, "SEE!" I told her I had to go.

Then to my horror, she somehow remembered that I had promised to give her a ride to her beautician's the next day. Yea, Yea, I'll call you in the morning, but I have to go now. She finally got out. I drove home thinking, "So this is freedom?" I'd better brace myself for the single life.

Trying to be a man of my word, I called her late the next morning. I knew she would need plenty of time to sleep off the night before, so I waited as long as I could before her appointment. The phone rang and rang, and finally someone picked up the phone and dropped it onto the floor before even saying hello.

The phone was picked back up off the floor and this slow, hoarse, hung-over-sounding voice said "H-e-l-l-o?"

I said, "Hello, is this the town lush?"

Then the voice said, "Hold on - MOM!"

Then she got on the phone, sounding just fine.

"How do you feel this morning?" I asked.

She said, "Great."

I said, "You mean you're not hung over?"

"Oh, no," she said. "After you dropped me off, me and the kids ate pizza and I drank more beer!"

Just great. So over I went to take her to get her hair cut. I don't consider giving someone a ride to the beauty shop, a date.

We drove forever it seemed until we got to where she wanted to go. I decided to wait outside in the car. After a long wait, I decided to go in to see how much longer it was going to take. She was sitting in the chair with her hair wet, drinking another beer! I just went back to the car. It was an even longer trip back to her home. I didn't ask anyone else out for awhile.

Daddy's Girl

So my friend decided to fix me up with one of his clients. He had fixed me up before, so I should have known better. Anyway, this one sounded promising. We met at a popular restaurant, with my friend there to introduce us. Her name would have been perfect for a country music singer. She was wearing leather pants, which was a turn-off for me. She had long, straight hair and was in good shape, but needed makeup lessons. Her eyes bulged like a goldfish. She was assertive—too assertive. One of the first things she said was that she had told her daddy my name, where I was from, and if I tried anything, he was going to come after me with his gun. I said I thought she was a little old to still be dependent on daddy. Undaunted, she assured me she could take care of herself. I told her if she was so worried, I would have brought a criminal background sheet with me. Reluctantly, we proceeded to have dinner.

She candidly told me that she could out-lift every man at the gym in bench pressing. I expressed my doubt, stating that she was not a very large or bulky woman. She then had to show me her biceps, flexing her arms in a body-building pose. Despite her lack of estrogen, she went on to state how intelligent and successful she was. She also stated how lucky I was to be on a date with her, because most men couldn't handle her and were intimidated by her. I think she was confusing intimidation with being an obnoxious redneck.

I didn't say much after that—partly because I wasn't the least interested in her, and partly because I was afraid if I said or did something wrong, she would kick my balls into next week for no reason. She went on talking, but saying nothing. It was a good thing I didn't bring flowers. They would have wilted the first time she opened her mouth. We ended the date from inside the bar, with her telling me I just wasn't man enough for her. Somehow, I resisted the urge to go out and buy a truck with three-foot diameter wheels to restore my ego. Yes, she'll always be daddy's girl, because no one else would have her.

ANIMAL INSTINCT

I went back to the singles club again. It was the second time. This time it was a small event which was held at a local restaurant. Less than a hundred people were there. There was this incredibly hyper woman there who stood out among the rest. She was petite with a loud voice, like one of those cute small dogs that yap constantly. She seemed to be popular, as she had the attention of a small crowd. She had short auburn hair, freckles, and adorable dark eyes. She was one of those irresistibly cute women who you just wanted to hug. Someone, maybe one of her girlfriends, I don't remember, asked her how she coped with being single.

Her reply was, "Batteries, lots of batteries!"

Now who could resist a woman like that? I just had to meet her. So I introduced myself and by the end of the evening I had asked her out. We met for dinner a week or so later. She turned out to be a veterinarian. She had dogs—huge dogs. I think they were Newfoundlands, or something like them. She had a great personality. To my recollection, she was in the process of changing or joining a new practice in the community.

I don't recall many other details, but I think she had been burned recently and wasn't ready for any commitments. I probably came on too strong or something, but it was a nice date at any rate. I think my friend dropped in on us to check her out. Curiosity had gotten the best of him. After he left, I walked her out to her car. No kiss goodnight; just that irresistible hug I had wanted since the first time I had seen her. I called her a couple of times after that, but she was too "busy" to make any plans. With veterinarians like her, I can understand how the term "lucky dog" came about. If I were a dog, I would contemplate running out in front of a car just to get to see her!

Whiny Dancer

This date could have been left out altogether. It was uneventful and forgettable. I just couldn't resist the title. She was a ballet instructor. We were set up on a blind date by my friend 1-900. Whiny Dancer and I met, along with 1-900 and her boyfriend. She was very pretty with long blonde hair. We seemed to converse well, or at least she was good at faking being interested. I thought she was fairly interesting, but slightly stand-offish. We talked for a couple of hours, and it was easier having mutual friends there. I asked her if she would like to see me again, and she gave me her number. 1-900 later gave me positive feedback from her, so I attempted to contact her. I don't really remember if we talked by phone or not, or whether I just developed a relationship with her answering machine. At any rate, there was no further date. I guess she was just being polite in the presence of company.

She later ended up working for a department store that I used to work for. I still had mutual friends there and I began to hear interesting stories about her. It turned out that she was fairly spoiled and made demanding requests of others. I decided to drop in on her one day on the spur of the moment, while I was in the area for a friendly visit. It was probably close to a year since we had met, but that didn't matter to me. I had recently been contacting everyone and anyone I had known or been introduced to within reason. Actually, Beacon and I had recently broken up for the first time and I was desperately seeking a revenge date. In reality, the man Beacon left me for had bought her a bouquet of flowers that cost more than my paycheck, and then he later bought a Porsche for her to "borrow." So in my mind, dating a ballet instructor seemed like good revenge. It conjured up images of being very flexible and acrobatic, if you know what I mean.

So I walked up to the cosmetics counter where she worked. She saw me coming and literally ducked down behind the counter and began to act busy. Another co-worker approached me and asked if she could help me. I said no, I was just here to visit Whiny Dancer. The co-worker informed me that she was busy and asked me to come back later. How humiliating. Not only did she recognize me from a distance, but she also literally hid from me as if I had the plague or something. Gee, so much for first impressions. She couldn't even tell me to my face to get lost. She sent someone else to do it for her. No private dances for me. She went from tu-tu's to tisk tisk, but I was able to quickly laugh about it and move on.

A Kiss Is Still a Kiss

I was at another one of those incredible singles club parties. They have played a major role in several chapters of this book. The band was great and hundreds of people were there. It was semi-formal and took place during the holiday season. I cruised around the ballroom, visiting my regular friends. At some point early in the evening, I noticed this gown. It was an incredibly beautiful and elegant strapless gown. It was black with pearl white silk edging around the top. She was facing away from me, and had long, thick blonde hair. I had to tell her that she was the best-dressed woman in the place.

So I approached her from behind, tapped her on her bare shoulder, and said, "Excuse me."

She turned around and I was a little taken aback. She wasn't particularly attractive, but not unattractive either. She was average looking, with a rough complexion. I guess I was expecting Miss America to go along with that gown. I told her she was the best-dressed woman there, and complimented her on her taste in clothing. She thanked me, and incredibly, she told me she thought I was the best-dressed man there! Now what are the odds of two strangers in a crowded place thinking each other is the best dressed?

Although I meant what I said, she looked out of place in that dress. We moved out into the lobby because she wanted to smoke, and it was hard to hear over the band. Awkwardness aside, she was real. She was so comfortable with herself and unpretentious. I was drawn to her. We talked for awhile and enjoyed each other's company. Our interest in each other peaked to the point where we agreed to see each other again. She gave me her number and then we went back to join the party.

Our first date happened to be on New Year's Eve. I was staying at one of the finest hotels in town, where ironically I had stayed the year before for the same holiday. She was dressed down from the last time I had seen her of course, but she still looked nice. We discussed our lives and loves. I was surprised to learn that she had been in the army. Although she was friendly, I detected a tone that kept her distant from me somewhat. After a nice dinner, she decided she wouldn't be staying the night with me. She did want to come up and see the room, out of curiosity. Oh, so close! Up in the room, before she left, I asked her if we could kiss. She accepted with a warm smile, and we embraced.

But it was no ordinary kiss! Our mouths made love. Her lips weren't necessarily soft, as you would expect a woman's lips to be, but they had this incredible texture that tingled and excited my senses. Every nerve ending in my mouth came alive. It was as if she had lit a fuse that burned its way down my spine. It wasn't hurried or sloppy. Our tongues conducted a symphony of feelings that overwhelmed my senses. My whole body tingled. I could feel it all the way down to my toes. I've never felt anything like that kiss. She left me numb. It was literally better than losing my virginity.

Knees wobbling, I escorted her back down through the lobby and out to her car. We said goodbye through her car window. We agreed to meet for brunch the next morning before I left town. Before she could back out, I just couldn't resist leaning in for another kiss. Again, it was unbelievable. She drove away and I just stood there in the parking lot, reduced to a mere speed bump. For the rest of the evening, my mouth just didn't feel the same. It was like having gone to a dentist who gives you a shot of Novocain and it takes hours to wear off.

After a sleepless night, I went over to her house the next morning. I presented her with the hospitality gift basket and wine from my room. She had a Jacuzzi on her back deck that sent my imagination into overdrive. She explained to me about some personal issues she was dealing with. I tried to be comforting and positive to no avail.

I even invited her to an upcoming Jimmy Buffett concert. She was tempted, but turned me down. (I thought women would go out with almost anyone just to go to a Jimmy Buffett concert!) Something was wrong. The magic was gone, or maybe it was never there to begin with. Then she got around to telling me she had also met someone else that night at the party. She assured me that nothing was wrong with me, but she wanted to pursue him instead. I felt like she didn't even give me a chance. Oh, yea, did I mention that I lived 100 miles away and he was local? Gee, I bet that had something to do with it.

Up until now, I had never seemed to meet Ms. Right in my hometown. I thought of her often for a long time afterwards, wondering who's kissing her now, and did she have the same effect on him. I'm thankful for that simple gesture she gave me. I'll remember it for the rest of my life.

Just Kill Me

Well, here goes another disaster. Once again, a co-worker set us up. She was a well-respected, older co-worker of mine. She stated that she had a niece who was single and not much older than me. She lived in a town about forty-five minutes away, and she was a redhead (my favorite hair color, in case you haven't guessed by now). Always up for adventure, I accepted the challenge. We agreed to meet downtown one evening in front of a landmark of some sort. We described our vehicles for recognition. I got there before she did, of course (Rule #1: Never leave a woman waiting alone), and soon she pulled up. We got out and introduced ourselves, and she agreed to take me in her vehicle since she knew her way around the town.

She was average looking, despite the red hair, and carried a few extra pounds. She was very nervous, and rightly so. I forget how many years she told me it had been since she had been on a date, but it was something incredible like ten or twelve. That was hard to imagine. She wasn't bad looking or anything, so I wondered why no one had asked her out in such a long time. In a way, I felt sorry for her, but not too sorry, because she was fairly wealthy.

She wanted to show me her condo, so we went over for a look. I began to get a little nervous, thinking it had been so long since she had been with a man that she might rape me or something. She had a fairly small but nice place. As we were about to leave, I asked her if it had been that long since she had dated, did that mean it had been that long since she kissed a man? She said yes, and began to blush. I said she had waited long enough. I asked her if she wanted one now instead of waiting until after dinner. She laughed out loud and got embarrassed again. We kissed and she was very thankful.

She had just bought a house, and she also wanted to show it to me. As we approached one stoplight that was red, she was oblivious to it. She just kept nervously talking about something.

I said, "The light is red."

She just kept gabbing.

"The light is red!" I stated again.

She had no clue. I grabbed the door handle and squeezed it tightly as she had no intention of stopping.

We cruised right through that light, and I stated, "Did you know we just ran a red light?"

Then suddenly, it registered in her brain. This embarrassed her and she apologized over and over for it. I was beginning to believe it really had been that long since she was on a date. It could have been the last one for both of us. Maybe it would have put me out of my misery that was forthcoming.

Anyway, we drove to a nice neighborhood and pulled in the drive. It was a large, older home that needed some work. It was unfurnished and in need of updating. We toured the inside and she told me about her plans for it and asked for my opinion. Her plans would take considerable expense, but I'm sure it was going to look beautiful when it was finished.

Meanwhile, we had a choice for dinner between two restaurants. I chose one of them, and she agreed. A short while later, we pulled into the wrong restaurant. Oh boy, things weren't looking up at this point. I said I thought we had agreed to go to the other restaurant. Again, the light bulb went on, and she embarrassingly apologized. It was okay with me, but I was beginning to wonder about her. Gee, did one kiss have that affect on her? Was I that great of a kisser? Or, was she just so desperate that anyone would have had that affect on her? Now I know why we are supposed to wait until after dinner for these foolish things.

Over dinner, the topic of conversation took a turn for the worse. I don't remember how the subject came up, but at some point, she began to get morbid. She asked me if I had ever considered suicide.

Horrified, I said no (ok, maybe at one point during my divorce, but that's not the point here). She said that she had, and then she asked me if I were ever considering it, how I would do it. I said I didn't know, and tried to change the subject. She was persistent and pressed me for an answer.

Finally I said, "I don't know. Maybe I'd use a gun."

Suddenly, she became adamant about how that would not be the correct way to do it. She went on to explain what a mess it would make and how bad it would be for the person who found you.

"Unless, of course," she said, "you shot yourself in the shower. That way, the mess would be easier to clean, and you wouldn't stain any carpet or curtains, or anything." Then she added, "So, what would be your next choice of methods?"

I sat there with my mouth hanging open I'm sure, and didn't know what to say or do. After a moment, I said I didn't know and I was uncomfortable discussing the subject. She was persistent. She wasn't joking. Her intonation was serious. She demanded to know how else I would choose to do it.

In exasperation, I threw up my hands and said, "Okay, how about running the car in the garage?"

"Oh, no!" she said. "Sometimes the gasses don't fully kill you and you can end up in a coma at the hospital for years!"

She went on about how hard that would be on the family and friends.

"Come on now, how else would you do it?"

At this point, I told her we were not having this conversation anymore. All I wanted to do was leave. I was ready to call a cab at that point.

She kept insisting, and wanted to know how I would do it.

Finally, I said, "Well, how would you do it?"

Elated, she said that she had been studying up on the subject and knew the best way! She excitedly told me that pills were the way to go—not just any pills—she knew the best ones to combine for the maximum effect. She stated the name of some medications I'd never heard of before. She seemed almost proud that she knew the best way to do the deed.

I began shaking at this point. I asked her please not to ever do any such thing. I told her help was available, counseling, etc. My heart was pounding wildly. I wanted nothing else to do with her, but I was also afraid to leave her. I lost my appetite. I think the subject finally changed, but I was in such shock I didn't hear much of what she said. The craziest things ran through my head. Was I somehow responsible for her actions? If I said or did the wrong thing, would she kill herself? Was I supposed to be the reason she wanted to live? What if she did it and I was the last person who saw her alive? Would I be a suspect or get arrested or something? I ended our dinner and told her to please take me back to my car. She drove me back without incident. Paralyzed with indecision, I offered her a hug goodnight. Oh my God, I thought, is this the right thing to do? Talk about not knowing what to do, I gave her my number in case she needed to call. I literally expected her to call me in the middle of the night ready to do it.

The call never came that night. My co-worker was horrified that she had ever told me about her. She stated that she knew that her niece had dealt with problems in the past, but wasn't aware that she still had issues. I assured her that her niece's problems were still present and accounted for. The co-worker apologized profusely. I said it was okay, but someone better keep an eye on her. I called the lady a few days later, just to see if she was still alive. She was polite, but somewhat embarrassed. I even offered to visit her again if she needed me to. I didn't really want to, but I didn't know what else to say. She declined, stating she was doing fine. She thanked me again for the evening, and we wished each other well. I truly hope she's alive and well, and even married.

Cat Woman

We worked together, but in different departments. I had noticed her before, but nothing much beyond a passing "hello" had occurred for the first few months. Then one day, she wrote me a note. She asked me out to the movies because there was one playing that she wanted to see. She included her number, so I called, of course.

She was very cute, and incredibly petite with a perfectly proportioned sexy body. She had jet-black short hair that was thick and full and framed her face beautifully. She wore these cat-woman type glasses with a thick frame and pointed upper edges. She was one of those librarian types of fantasies. Behind those kinky glasses were the most beautiful blue eyes. She was very captivating, and I had wanted to get to know her better since I had first noticed her.

We planned a date for the following weekend. We met for an evening out and nice conversation, but the whole time, I noticed she was acting very nervous and kept looking around. She was paranoid that she would see someone she knew who would tell her ex-husband what she was doing. She and her ex were not on good terms, and there was a small child between them. I guess she was afraid that being on a date would somehow jeopardize her custody or something.

She was nice and friendly, but she was going through a rough divorce. She really wasn't ready for dating, but we agreed to be friends. We were the same age. I found out that she had dated much older men before, which was something we had in common, because I had dated much older women. After dinner, we went to see that movie she wanted to see, but it wasn't playing anymore. It didn't last long at the box office. So we decided to go rent a movie and watch it back at my place. We pulled in at the local Blockbuster, but again she hesitated to go in. She thought she saw someone she knew and wouldn't even get out of the car. I offered to go in and pick something out for us, but she just wanted to leave altogether. I drove her back to her car, and she followed me back to my place. When we got there, she insisted that she should park her car in my garage. Again, she didn't want anyone to see her car at my place, even though it was dark. This poor lady was as paranoid as she was pretty.

We went inside for awhile and talked some more. She wasn't interested in seeing anything from my movie collection because I didn't have anything with Marlon Brando in it. He was her favorite actor. As nice as she was, she really wasn't able to converse well for worrying about who had possibly seen us together that night. I felt kind of sorry for her. She obviously loved her child very much, and I don't blame her for trying to protect her. I asked for a kiss at the end of the evening, but she was unsure about that, too. So we just hugged and then she left.

I stayed in touch with Cat Woman for awhile and we met for lunch one time after that as friends. I wished her well, and eventually everything worked out for her divorce. Ironically, she is now married to a police officer. I guess he makes her feel safe.

Date.com

Her picture was the prettiest on the Internet dating service. I was completely enamored with her profile. I e-mailed her, and she responded. She had a beautiful and uncommon name; I wish I could mention it. Then we called each other. She seemed pleasant over the phone, but she was doubtful. So I gave her the number of one of my best female friends, and she called her. After that, she somewhat reluctantly agreed to meet. She lived about an hour away. It was on my birthday, so I had lunch at one of my favorite restaurants in a town near where we would meet. We met in a small coffee shop that afternoon. I brought some pictures along for conversation. I arrived before she did, and I was the only one in the place.

After a nervously long wait, a Lexus pulled up and parked right beside my car. I knew it was her before I even saw her. She got out, fixed her hair, and taking a deep breath, stretched tall and adjusted her thin, Carolina blue sweater. She looked even better in person. And oh, what breasts! They were huge, full, and perfect. They looked back at me as if to say, "Catch us if you can" (We guys think that's what most breasts are saying to us, anyway). Her waist looked like it was about eighteen inches around. She had beautiful medium-length brown hair with lots of body to it. She was petite with a healthy, natural kind of beauty. I was so intimidated just seeing her that I broke into a laugh thinking how disappointed in me she would be; a good story to share with her friends. Did I mention the breasts?

Then she entered. Our eyes met, and she smiled. I offered my hand and she took it obligingly. I proceeded to give her a present. She had mentioned in an earlier phone conversation that she liked plants. Not knowing anything about them, I went to a posh plant store earlier and asked for help. They steered me toward something called Antherium.

I was so nervous when we met that I said, "Here's a plant for you. It's an Anthrax!"

We both laughed over that one.

After the usual pleasantries and pictures, things took a more serious note. We moved outside to the patio. I discussed my divorce and how it had affected me. Then she opened up to me about her situation. She wept when telling me the story of her husband's death. I held her hand, so delicate and soft. She told me while at his death bed, he tried to speak but didn't have the energy. So he began to spell out her name. I believe she said he got through the first three letters, and that was the last thing he did. He was trying to tell her she was the one, even though his ex-wife was also there with them.

Her love died completely intact with him. No bitter dissention or divorce. It was something beautiful within such a tragedy—a silver lining on a dark cloud. A couple of hours went by, I guess. I showed her some boxers I had bought earlier that day. Smooth move, idiot. She complimented me on the way I was dressed. She even checked out my shoes. Women do that, you know. She had to go pick up her daughter, but the date wasn't over yet.

We hugged goodbye temporarily at the vehicles. She fit well in my arms. She was so petite and beautiful. I was glad it wasn't over. We agreed to meet a couple of hours later at a movie theater. I had some time to kill, so I ate dinner at a nearby shopping center. I called my best friend LA, the one she had called for a "reference."

When she answered, I simply stated, "LA, when we hang up, I want you to do me a favor. Get on your knees and pray for me that she is the one."

Knowing me well, LA just said something like, "Yea, yea, here we go again."

Date.com and I met later at the theater. Her little girl was with her. How precious she was! She had long brown hair and big brown eyes, just like her mom. We watched some campy kid's movie about a dog from outer space. Periodically throughout the film, Date.com would lean over to whisper conversation in my ear. She was so close to me—cheek-to-cheek—as close as you could get without touching. I could smell her hair. I found it somewhat erotic, there in the darkened theater. To this day, I don't know what she said. Towards the end, her daughter grew tired and climbed into her lap. I could *feel* the love between them, and I was there with them. Now, if only I could somehow manage to be there *for* them.

The movie ended and we walked out to her car. We shook hands good-night. No hug. No kiss. I wasn't expecting one because of her child. But oh, how I wanted that kiss! This wasn't just infatuation; I had actually fallen for her by now. I don't remember the ride home. I ecstatically called LA again. All the way home, I savored the thought of one of my best birthdays ever. The next thing I remember was being in the shower late that night. I prayed to God that she was the one. She made sense to me. I thought she would be the reason my previous relationships had failed. I felt I had enough love for both of them—her and her child.

I called the next day. She was in the grocery store. She tactfully explained to me that I lived too far away to have a practical relationship. She was also disappointed with my job. (A stop-gap job at the time between career changes.) She was appalled that with my background and education I was doing what I was to survive. I thought it might have showed character or something. You know, the old, "I'm not beneath that" routine.

After probably what was a desperate plea to see her again, she said goodbye. She was in the express lane. I was in shock. She wasn't rude. She was just being realistic. I prayed for her and her daughter every day for six months. At that time, I e-mailed her again. She never responded.

At the time of this writing, her photo is still on the dating website. I look at it occasionally, wondering "what if?" I wonder who is kissing her now. I wonder why my love was never enough. Oh, well. My faith rests on someday receiving an explanation. My problems were temporary; my personality wasn't. If she only knew how different things are for me now.

Private Eyes

My friend, Genius, called me up one evening and said her friend had cancelled at the last minute for some sort of conference on menopause and estrogen. She asked me to go with her and I had five minutes to get ready. Menopause and estrogen? Why would I want to go to such a meeting? Genius then reminded me that I would probably be the only guy there. Let's see now; me in a room full of women. Hum...Works for me! So off we went to learn about the change of life for women. We were late and snuck around to the back row. For two hours, we sat on hard metal fold-out chairs, listening to a subject that could have not been more boring for me. Genius owed me for that one. There was one lady in particular whom I noticed at the meeting; the only really attractive woman there. She sat in the front row and I just stared at her long beautiful hair most of the time. It turned out that Genius knew the woman, and a few days later she contacted her to see if she was dating anyone. Genius had been friends with this woman when she was married, and now she was separated. (Foreshadowing here, folks.)

It turned out she wasn't seeing anyone at the time. She stated that she had also noticed me at the meeting and would like to meet me. We exchanged e-mail addresses and she contacted me. Her e-mail was a little shocking to me. This woman had noticed many details about me at the meeting—what I was wearing, how I behaved, my every move, it seemed. Anyway, she was quite attractive and sexy so we decided to meet. She lived about thirty minutes away so we got our directions and plans down for the meet. We exchanged photos to help remind and recognize each other for our date.

I drove to her town and we met at a pizza parlor. I stood by the door waiting for her to arrive. I was in one of my aggressive moods that night, so when she walked in, I gave her a big hug and a smile. I told her I was glad to meet her and how good she looked. She said the same, and I knew it was going to be a good date. We had dinner and talked. It was an upbeat and cheerful discussion through the meal, and my interest in her grew. After dinner, it was still early and we didn't want the date to end. The town was very small, so the only place to go was a Waffle House. So I followed her there—bright lights, twenty-four-hour service, and a jukebox. How romantic. We had the place to ourselves, so we took a seat and continued our conversation.

However, something happened on the way to that Waffle House. The woman I had met at the pizza parlor was now someone else. She began to tell me about how her husband had abused her and her daughter so badly. I asked her why she stayed with him so long if it was that bad. She didn't have a good answer, but eventually she found the courage to leave him. I asked her what she did for a living, and she said she sold real estate. That's a respectable profession. I asked her which firm she worked for, and she stated she was an independent. Even better, I thought. Then she began to explain to me that she didn't *really* have a license. She just bought and sold houses for profit. I asked her how she knew which houses to buy and how she was so lucky to turn them over so quickly. She said God told her which houses to buy.

Okay, there's a moment in some dates where things turn differently. This was that moment. She went on to explain how she had divine visions or something to that effect, on which houses to buy and sell. I didn't really understand what she was trying to say, and I didn't want to, either. Then she explained how she thought it would be best if we were just friends, and how she wasn't ready for a relationship. Oh, well, I thought. You can't win them all. Still feeling confident, I walked her out to her car with my arm around her.

In an effort to change her mind, I said to her, "It's going to be hard to just be your friend." (Translation: I want your body, and then we can be friends.)

We hugged goodbye at the car, and she said she would like to see me again. I walked away, but after a few steps I stopped and turned around. I thought to myself, Wow, she was sexy! I said outloud, "What the hell?" and walked back to her. I grabbed her in my arms and kissed her ever so passionately. (A passionate kiss at a Waffle House? Yes, it's possible.)

She laughed and said, "That was great the way you did that."

I confidently drove home thinking I had sealed the deal on a second date. After all, who needs love? I just needed companionship, and a good-looking, sexy woman was just the ticket; even if she was a little loony.

The next day, I e-mailed her, thanking her for the date and expressing my wishes to see her again. To my surprise, she e-mailed back an unfriendly message stating that she wasn't ready for anything and that she thought it best not to see me again. I pondered over how to respond, so after awhile I wrote her back. I was aggressive again, stating how I wanted to kiss her "ever so passionately" again and how we could take it slow if she wanted.

She e-mailed back an even harsher message that made it perfectly clear that we wouldn't see each other again. Ouch! Okay, I've been humiliated before, so one more time wouldn't kill me. It's hard not to take it personally when you're rejected. Why did she enjoy the kiss goodnight? Why did she say she wanted to see me again if she really didn't?

Well, a couple of days later, Genius called me with some shocking news. It turned out that the woman wasn't exactly *legally* separated. So I had just had a date with and kissed a married woman. Then came the bad news. Genius had been friends with both the woman and her husband when they were married. The husband called Genius on the phone and wanted to know who I was. She asked him how he knew about me. He stated that his *private investigator* had intercepted our e-mails and he knew all about our date, and especially about the passionate kiss. He wanted to know whom this guy was that was kissing his wife and he wasn't happy about it.

93

Just great. Now there were two lunatics who hated me. What a great way to lose sleep. I laid in bed that night wondering if we were followed on our date. Were we spied on? What if there were photos? Would the "Waffle House romance" be in the newspaper? I could just see myself in their divorce court hearing. "Ladies and gentlemen of the jury, here's proof this man's a home wrecker," as the lawyer holds up a photo of us kissing under the bright yellow sign.

That evening, I went over to Genius's house to talk about this whole deal and how freaked out I was about it. Well, just when you think it couldn't get worse, the doorbell rang. It was him—the husband. He had printouts of my e-mails in his hand. Genius was quick on her feet and introduced me only as her neighbor. No name was mentioned. He actually shook my hand, and didn't have a clue who I was. I stated I had to go and somehow left unscathed. That was the longest three steps to the front door in my life. He tried to get info from her about me. However, she was a real trooper and told him she couldn't get a hold of me or something. I really can't remember what she said she had told him. I kept a low profile for the next few days. Gee, one date can almost ruin your whole life.

Size Matters

It's probably happened to most of us. She looked fine from the pictures she e-mailed me. She had long blonde hair and a warm smile. We talked on the phone a couple of times. She had plans for the east coast, but I was going to be in her town in a couple of weeks on business. So we planned a date. It was bound to happen sooner or later on one of my illustrious dates. She must have weighed well over 300 pounds. I couldn't believe how tremendous she was. I tried not to show any dismay, and was polite to her throughout the dinner. She was fairly pleasant, but I was glad to see our interests went in different directions.

I walked her back to her car, contemplating how to react if she wanted a kiss. I decided just to give her a hug, but that turned out to be a challenge in itself. I couldn't even begin to get my arms around her. My hands barely made it to the back of her shoulders. It was the most awkward hug I had ever endeavored. Oh, my God, how do these people have sex? I wasn't *even* about to find out as I bolted for the car. She tried to contact me several times after that, but I was "unavailable." Sometimes, you wonder what happened on a date, and what you did or said wrong. But she was bound to know. I guess being polite just led her on. I truly hope someone loves her for who she is and I wish her well.

Cher

Ah yes, the wine dinner. I was asked to fill in only after a cancellation—a friend of a friend type of deal. It was a private wine tasting/dinner, invitation only, at one of the most exclusive restaurants anywhere. Was I interested in attending a $125.00 a plate dinner at no charge? Why, that's better than a room full of post-menopausal women any day! Wild sex couldn't have kept me away. We were chauffeured to the event, but not in a limo. Who cares, anyway?

About fifty people or so were in attendance. While we were waiting to be seated, an appetizer buffet was available, complete with a chef preparing fresh crepes. A hostess was making rounds serving foie gras on a silver platter. That shit's for the birds (pun intended).

In walked some acquaintances of our group. Introductions and first impressions were made. With them was a rather tall, slender woman with freckles who strongly resembled Cher. I wasn't impressed with her at first, but she grew on me throughout the evening. She wasn't glamorous or pretentious, but she was comfortable with herself. She had a natural kind of innocence and curiosity. She was tall and thin, with this incredibly curly long, jet-black hair. We were finally seated for the dinner; I forget how many courses it was. I sat next to my friend, and Cher sat at the other end of a table for about ten. I'm not a wine fan, so I gave all my tastings to my friend. I ordered mixed drinks between courses, increasing my portion of the tab to even more astronomical heights. The meal was incredible. Throughout the evening, Cher and I exchanged occasional glances.

Finally, it was time for dessert. People were beginning to mingle and loosen up. Then she came over and sat next to me.

I said, "I was hoping you would sit beside me for dinner."

She said, "I'm sitting beside you *now*."

We exchanged similar flirtatious banter back and forth for a few moments. Then we talked honestly and openly for awhile. I felt comfortable with her. During our conversation, I inadvertently ate the last tuxedo strawberry. She had wanted it. So I offered to let me make it up to her by asking her to dinner.

Feeling especially suave under the atmosphere, I said to her, "Would you do me the honor of joining me for dinner?"

She accepted. That was the best dessert of all!

A week or so later, I stopped in at her workplace and asked her about dinner. She didn't seem too enthused, but agreed. I picked her up that weekend. She was a very practical, no nonsense lady with an irresistible smile. She was the type of woman you would lose every argument with. But still, I managed to blow it. I must have had too much on my mind or something, because I was unable to concentrate on what she was saying long enough to intelligently respond. It was as if we were speaking two different languages. I was a different man than the one she had met at the wine dinner. On top of that, I managed to insult her job. Needless to say, there was no kiss goodnight on that date. I called a few days later and apologized for being such a jerk. She said she would go out with me again as friends, so we arranged another meeting for drinks one evening. I found a place in town that made the tuxedo strawberries and was planning a surprise for her. She stood me up. She actually called the restaurant while I was there to say she was feeling sick. The phone was at the hostess's station by the front door. How humiliating. Everyone knew what was going on. I just walked out the front door after I hung up. Her revenge was appropriate, I guess.

Despite that, I wish her well as she adjusts to a new town and a new life. I have no hard feelings towards her. She's a very decent person and I'm sure she will succeed in life and with her career. I missed out on developing a potential friendship with her. Success will be her revenge for guys like me who imply she wasn't good enough, although that wasn't my intention. But I did use a poor choice of words that night. Oh, well. I may drop in on her again some day and ask her where I fall on her list of worst dates. Maybe she should write a book or something.

The Look

About one in every 1,000 or so women you see, one just stands above the rest. They have the "look." It's not that this particular lady was more worthy than others left out of this book, but more that she is a symbol that represents the others I've occasionally crossed paths with.

She was a classic beauty, poised and refined. Her hair was long and thick, and her skin was flawless. I saw her from across the room at a luncheon. Afterwards, I asked a lady she had been talking with who she was. I got her info and approval to call a few days later. She seemed pleasant over the phone, as they all do. We decided to meet for lunch.

The date was awkward. It went nowhere fast. I was probably too old for her, or maybe I wasn't "worldly" enough for her, or both. I lost our game of "been there, done that." Then again, I never reveal all my cards on the first date, either. We shared one funny moment, but it was more like nervous laughter. We hugged goodbye and I asked her if I could contact her.

She said, Yes."

I said, "Really?"

Again, she said "Yes."

So a few days later, I called her, and she politely told me that she wasn't interested. I wasn't surprised, but I wish she could have spared me the phone call. Why didn't she just say that in person? Certainly she was cultured enough to tactfully tell me to get lost. Or, maybe I should have known she was just being polite. The games people play.

She was nice, but I haven't dwelled on her—a shooting star without a wish. No "What If?" I don't even regret not kissing her. I guess I'm getting a little more practical with my perspectives. Now, only 999 more to go…

To summarize the dating lessons I've learned so far, here are some reminders to adhere to:

Dating Tip #1. Listen to your heart.
Dating Tip #2. Red flags are your friends.
Dating Tip #3. The bigger the breasts, the more forgiving us men can be.
Dating Tip #4. Breast size really doesn't matter.
Dating Tip #5. Intelligence does.
Dating Tip #6. When you exchange photos, make sure they show more than just the face.
Dating Tip #7. Don't say *Call me* when you mean *Get lost.*
Dating Tip #8. If you're only separated, you're not ready to date anyone.
Dating Tip #9. If you're already married, one night can ruin everything.
Dating Tip #10. If they're rich, ignore all of the above tips.

Part IV:
Trivial Pursuits

Most of these experiences never really led to any dates—a few close calls, but not quite there. I have pursued some of these women for years. Others I knew from college and haven't seen or heard about since. Some of these women probably wouldn't remember me if they tried. Yet, they impressed me enough to remember them, at least for this book. Some of them were married at the time I pursued them. Some of them I would marry tomorrow if I had the chance. Some of them are just plutonic friends or acquaintances. And some of them I just plain lust for.

These women have made things interesting in my life (and in my dreams). I can laugh and joke about it with some of them. They are an endless tease. Inside, I've longed for at least a chance with them—an "ideal" in my mind that in reality probably wouldn't work out. I guess I figure I can sort of "wear them down" over time or something. Like maybe they'll get desperate enough someday to give me that chance. It's a kind of hope that keeps me going and helps me feel that maybe all is not lost during times when I'm down. Thank you, ladies, for the fun, the friendship, and the fantasy.

FAIR GAME

It was orientation day during my first weekend at college. There was a cookout on the main lawn area in front of one of the dorms. I had only met a few people, but immediately I noticed a beautiful girl who stood out among the crowd. I made it a point to "accidentally" sit beside her. As we ate ice cream in the grass, I noticed she was wearing a Band-Aid on one finger.

So as a conversation starter, I said, "How did you hurt your finger?"

She held up her other hand; the one without the Band-Aid. To my dismay, one finger had been severed about half way. She said it happened in a bicycle accident as a child. I apologized and told her I had not noticed that finger, but I was talking about the other one, which was the truth.

She was from a small town in the eastern part of the state. Her eyes were crystal blue against her sandy blonde hair. She was friendly and polite. We talked for awhile and then went about our separate ways. I felt I at least knew her well enough to say hello around campus now. Meanwhile, one of my other new guy friends turned out to be the biggest, most obnoxious prep on campus. He had more button-down shirts than anyone else on campus—most of them were pink.

During that first week of classes, he approached me in the hall one day and said, "Come here and I'll show you the prettiest girl on campus."

We proceeded down the hall. He pointed her out through the classroom window and said, "Check out that beauty!"

I said, "Yea, I've already met her."

That cooled his jets for awhile.

Our friendship remained mostly plutonic throughout the semester. I think I asked her to a dance or something, and she politely turned me down. She later dated this hip guy who played the drums. I remember being jealous of him, but we spoke to one another occasionally. I guess I could say she set the stage for my "ideal woman" at that time.

Flip

She was also one of the first people I met at college. She was petite and full of life with a smile bigger than she was. Laughter and humor seemed to always be with her. We were in a couple of classes and a play together. We sat beside each other in one class. One day we were watching a film. There was a scene that showed the ancient ruins of Greece.

She leaned over to me in the dark and whispered, "I've been there!"

"Cool," I stated.

The very next scene was of outer space with planets and stars.

Not to be out done, I leaned over to her and whispered, "I've been there!"

She laughed out loud and we both got in trouble for disrupting the class.

I had an incurable crush on her, fueled by almost daily interaction in and out of class. We probably couldn't have seen each other more if we had been dating. It wasn't an earth-moving experience to be around her. It was more like having an idea friend that you wanted to take one step further. She got married to a pilot soon after graduation. To this day, when I think of her, I still see her dancing and singing in a play we were in together.

Here's to Ewe

Ah, the college life! (The first time.) I really don't remember how we met. (Sorry!) She was tall, thin, and delicately feminine. She had very long strawberry blonde beautiful hair, and big doe eyes. She was the Celine Dion type. We never established a dating relationship as boyfriend-girlfriend; we just sort of hung out as friends. I guess this relationship was mostly in my head. (Okay, I was young. Give me a break.) Later on in the semester, she met some guy she wanted to date. He had long hair and played the guitar or something—not exactly the career type by my standards. What she saw in him, I don't know. So in an attempt to thwart disaster, I decided to tell her how I felt.

We went out one night and bought some wine and then went "parking." (There was NOWHERE to go in this town, believe me.) I'm not a wine person, but I figured what the heck and went for it.

So I spilled my guts and she said something like, "How sweet, but I really like this other guy."

We had been drinking the wine, so I figured I'd play the sympathy card next. I asked her if I could have a goodbye kiss. She obliged. I was expecting a quick "get-it-over-with" kiss, but to my surprise, it was long, tender, and meaningful. I still remember that kiss. I think she ended up marrying that guy. I wonder how long that lasted.

Jeans

Later on in college, I lived in the coolest apartment in town. It was private, beautiful, and an astronomical $300.00 per month. My neighbors were two girls who roomed together. Both of them were beautiful but one was all American and good looking. She looked like she could have been on the cover of a Beach Boys album. She was sweet and wholesome with a healthy look about her. She had long hair with body and clear skin. She was kind of tall with an average-to-slender build. We all three became friends and hung out together occasionally. One time when I was sick, they brought me hot soup.

Another time, we went to an antique auction together, and one of them won the door prize. It was a breadbox. I even got to know her family as they visited regularly. Then one day near the end of the semester, I decided to confess my crush on Jeans to her roommate. She assured me that Jeans didn't feel the same way about me, but tried to let me down easily. I'm glad I didn't confess my feelings directly to Jeans. I left after that semester to "find" myself. I soon realized that although Jeans was an ideal fantasy to me, her roommate was more of a practical match for me. Maybe I should have pursued her instead.

Anyway, we lost touch for awhile, but a couple of years later, I heard she was getting married. A co-worker at the time told me about it, so I crashed the wedding, uninvited. She and her family were glad to see me and welcomed me there. It was good to see them again, and I wished her well. I was really happy for her. She didn't seem to have the same effect on me anymore. I hope she remained married to him to this day.

Sunrise

I had survived a season on Palm Beach. (The OFF-season.) It was time to go back north and I wanted to say goodbye to the only friend I had made on the island. She lived in my complex. Or should I say, I lived in hers. Sunrise had long, dark curly hair and a wonderful smile. She was tall and lanky with a good sense of humor and a goofy personality. We ran into each other almost daily and usually stopped to talk. On my last evening there, we were having a particularly in-depth conversation about life as the night grew late. Neither one of us was sleepy, so we came up with the idea to just stay up all night and watch the sunrise over the water. She pulled up a lounge chair out on the patio and got cozy for the event, which was only a couple of hours away by then. I kept telling her that we needed to move out to the beach, but she said she wanted to stay by the intercoastal. It took me awhile to convince her that we were facing west and the sun rose over the ocean behind us from the east. She was such a goofball, but I finally convinced her to go to the beach or we would miss it altogether. So we drove the short distance over by the beach, just as the sky was beginning to get light. The actual beachfront was all private property, so I just pulled my car over to the side of the road into the sand. We sat there for about an hour watching the beautiful sky come to life before us. It was well worth the wait.

We were both sleepy by now, so we started to go back to the complex. However, we didn't get very far when I realized we were stuck in the sand. The wheels just kept spinning, which dug us even deeper into a rut. I had to get out and push while she hit the gas. I couldn't get much traction in the sand and kept slipping myself. By now we were causing a scene and people were just beginning to wake up. I just knew the owners of the million dollar estate we were stuck in front of, were going to call the authorities for trespassing if we didn't make it out of there soon. I had to run and get seashells for traction, and we finally got it back on the road. It was a disastrous ending to an otherwise touching goodbye.

Meanwhile, back at my place, I slept until noon. Then I packed up the car and headed for a final lunch at my favorite place, Chuck and Harold's. Afterwards, I would bid my final farewell, as if anyone cared. Although the island had taken its toll on me, there was one last thing I wanted to do. I had to have one last stroll down Worth Avenue, with its tiled canine drinking fountains and twenty dollar cab fares. (This was a long time ago.)

I went past the Taboo, where I spotted the "Prize Pulitzer" one evening at dinner. I walked past Petite Marmite, where I had also once imbibed the island's finest fare. After awhile, I returned to my car, only to find a parking ticket on the windshield. How dare they give me a ticket! You mean my Camaro didn't fit in along side the Excaliburs? Now I was angry. That was the last straw. Instead of quietly leaving town officially ostracized, I decided I was going out with a bang. I'll ruffle their truffles, by golly! I cranked down the windows and cranked up the stereo, full blast. I had the perfect commemorative song on cassette, *Street Life* by the Crusaders. So I took off down Worth Avenue, trying to offend as many people as possible (I had never really *tried* to offend the natives; it just sort of came naturally). Stares and dropped jaws appeared as the four-barrel carburetor kicked in, leaving my semi-permanent marks on the street.

As if that weren't enough, I headed straight for The Breakers—no more sneaking in on the side by the condos. I headed straight down the main entrance and around the fountain, with my CB radio antenna whipping wildly from the back. Boy, I sure showed them, huh? I tore that ticket in half and tossed it over the Flagler Bridge. I left with a newfound admiration for Cliff Robertson and Roxanne Pulitzer. In my mind, I could sort of identify with them now, after having been treated so unfairly.

Several months later, that ticket arrived in the mail. It had risen from the depths of the intercoastal waterways to haunt me again. Touché' for Palm Beach. You just can't win down there.

Bamboozled

This woman was a married co-worker whom I fell in lust with shortly after I met her. We grew closer as friends during our years together. She had this wild long hair that seemed to always be out of control. Her facial features were a bit awkward and out of balance. Her nose wasn't straight and her eyes were slightly crossed, but she was very sexy. She had a blunt personality and a wild spirit. She was the kind of person you wouldn't want for an enemy.

As time went by, she began to confide some of her marital problems to me. That's the first step in the wrong direction for co-workers. What she meant to say was that their problems were not insurmountable. What I heard was what I wanted to hear, and I took that to mean an opportunity for us. Blinded by lust, I tried to pursue this woman as surreptitiously as possible while at work. I took advantage of any opportunity I could to be with her.

We had a few lunches together and one time we even discussed sexual likes and dislikes. Then one day, I asked her to lunch because I knew it would be our last, at least as co-workers. I was going to be leaving the company and I decided this was the opportunity to express my feelings towards her. We discussed my future plans and I sought her advice and opinion. She was supportive and wished me well.

On the way back home, I began thinking about a carefully scripted and rehearsed speech that I would say to her. I thought it was pretty clever at the time. I began by telling her the story of how I had developed this crush on a married woman and needed her advice on how to handle it. I told her the reasons I liked this woman so much and about how attractive and wonderful she was.

After the build-up and praise, I said to her, "So what do you think? Should I tell her how I feel?"

She said no, I shouldn't. She went on to say that it would just cause problems and eventually hurt a lot of innocent people.

Then I stated, "Well, it's too late. I already have."

She asked me why I was asking her opinion, and wanted to know what the woman said.

To which I replied, "Well, she hasn't figured it out yet. It should hit her any minute now."

I thought she was going to jump out of the car.

She said something like, "Oh, my God, are you talking about me?"

I didn't say a word, but looked straight at her and simply nodded my head yes. She completely freaked out. She said her marital problems didn't mean she wanted a divorce, and that our conversations were not meant to lead me on. She stated she loved her husband and would be faithful to him.

When we got back to work, she literally jumped out of the car and ran into the building before I could even park my vehicle. I'm so glad I waited until my last day to tell her. The rest of the afternoon was awkward at best, as I tried to keep a low profile to hide my embarrassment. It was a futile attempt at an immoral plan to begin with. I'm glad it didn't work. Someone in these situations has to be strong, and thank goodness it was her, because I would have succumbed to any sort of favorable response. There would have been no future in it anyway, and she really wasn't even my type. If and when I ever end up with someone for the long run, I hope she is that strong if anything like that ever happens to her. Looking back on it now, I never even noticed the most attractive thing about her until after our friendship was over—her faithfulness.

Time Management

Believe it or not, this was another married woman at the same company I worked at with Bamboozled. Okay, two married women at the same company, at the same time? Well, I did admit that one was just lust. This one, though, was more. I was completely infatuated with her. She had it all: looks, intelligence, education, kindness, professionalism, and she was the perfect wife, mother, and Christian.

We worked and communicated together regularly. My respect for her grew over the years. Then one day she was helping me with a problem requiring her expertise. She was dressed particularly feminine that day. She wore a navy blue dress with a white collar and matching sleeves. She had on white hose and her hair and makeup were flawless. As she was explaining something to me, it just hit me. I had liked and respected her up until now, but I had never noticed how beautiful she was until this moment. She transformed before my eyes. I kept thinking, "Wow! She really looks beautiful!" I never heard a word she said. All I know is that she fixed the problem and went on her way. And my heart went right along with her.

I wouldn't call it love; I think it was just the height of admiration. Then again, I once told her that if anything ever happened to her husband, that I would marry her and raise her kids. That's a lot of admiration. I think I may have tried to propose to her one day when she secretly confessed to me in her office that she was a nymphomaniac. Now that's something every wife should tell a co-worker, of course.

I had also planned to have a "last lunch" with her that same week I was leaving. She declined by e-mail. I think she sensed that something was amiss. I responded by saying that was probably a smart move—leaving her to either wonder about or confirm her suspicions. Again, someone besides me was in control. I later had another co-worker tell me it was obvious that I was infatuated with her. She told me that I "came alive" whenever she was around. Gee, am I that obvious when I like someone? Do I walk into walls or something?

I now realize that these co-workers were my attempt to seek an "out" from my failing marriage. So I was left to deal with it on my own, the way it should be. Fear can drive us to seek solutions that avoid dealing with that fear. I believe that I played out an example of that theory.

Steal Away

This one was elusive. I had heard a lot about her, but it took quite awhile to finally meet her. I think it may have been because the only person I knew who could introduce me to her, may have been a little jealous of her. She thought I would be more interested in Steal Away than her. She would have been right except for one thing. Steal Away was more interested in herself than anyone else.

Finally, the day arrived when all three of us would meet and go out together. It was a spur-of-the-moment thing, and totally unplanned. We called and were invited to her condo for a visit.

After our introductions, the first thing I said to my friend was, "I thought you said she was cute?". However, before I could say the rest of my sentence, Steal Away was immediately offended and began telling me so in no uncertain terms.

I, being the suave guy I sometimes like to think I am, quickly made up for it by saying, "She's pretty, and there's a big difference."

That brought her down a notch or two. We conversed in the living room for a short while over a couple glasses of wine. She was quite attractive, but it soon became apparent why she had never been married. I don't think many men out there were good enough for her, and I certainly wasn't about to win her over. Then she decided to invite us to go see her perform at a local dinner theater play. It was close to the holidays and it was opening night for the Christmas performance. It was great how we walked into the crowded building without reservations and got a table up front, close to the stage. The performance was thoroughly entertaining. Steal Away was quite talented and professional. My friend and I were having a wonderful time enjoying dinner and the show.

Then at one point during the performance, she was supposed to invite an audience member to come up on stage and dance with her. Guess whom she chose? Yep, she came and got me by the hand, and almost had to drag me up on stage in front of a packed house. It was just me and her together on the stage. To make matters worse, this wasn't some sort of a romantic slow dance or anything. She had me put on a grass skirt in front of everyone and do the Hawaiian hula dance with her. I've never figured out why that was part of a Christmas show, but it was quite humiliating. (Dating Tip # 11: Never insult someone who has a position of power or authority over you.)

Up until then, it had been quite a pleasant evening. Afterwards, everyone told me I did a great job, but what were they supposed to say? All I wanted to do was leave as quickly as possible, which took quite awhile due to the crowds. Do you think I ever contacted this woman again? You guessed it.

Actually, I did see her again years later at the wedding of my friend's daughter. She was eating a plate of finger food. I politely spoke to her and simply offered to get her a drink.

She looked at me and said sharply, "I'm dating someone," and then she quickly turned and walked away. I tried to tell her I didn't mean it like that, but she was gone. Excuse the hell out of me, but I was only trying to be polite, with no intention of anything else. I'll bet she's still not married.

1~900

We met at a health club (A great place to meet women, by the way). We were next to each other on the treadmills when she struck up a conversation. She was tall with short blonde hair. She was very personable, cute, and sexy. We became acquaintances at the club and developed a friendship. She was dating some guy and we discussed relationships, among other things. She's the one who fixed me up with Whiny Dancer. She was very personable and fun to be around.

I don't recall exactly how we transitioned from acquaintances to friends, but soon we were calling and e-mailing frequently. I even visited her at work one time when I was there doing business in the same building.

We traded jokes back and forth, and laughed a lot. She complemented me on my sense of humor. Somewhere along the way, the e-mails began to get raunchy, and our conversations turned risqué. As things progressed, or should I say digressed, she began to send me sexy photos of herself in various stages of undress. However, she would cover critical parts with her hands, for instance. We also began to have what I guess they call "phone sex." We would begin to get each other off over the phone, describing ourselves and our likes and dislikes. One time, we actually mutually masturbated over the phone together to climax. I had never done anything like that before, but I found it very exciting. I left her sexy fantasy phone messages to which she admitted she succumbed to. She was by far the most sexually uninhibited woman I had ever known. She described things I had never heard of or even *imagined* doing. Oh, how I wanted her to try them on me! I stayed pretty worked up over her, most of the time. She could have easily become habit forming.

Then came the day when I invited her over to see my Christmas tree. She agreed and came over one evening. I'm not one to buy wine, but for some unknown reason, I happened to have some on hand that night. I think someone may have given it to me as a seasonal gift for some reason. As she sat on my couch sipping wine, we began to discuss sex. I actually showed her the bedroom, where we lingered for a moment pondering the possibilities. I told her she had a standing invitation to my bed. However, we behaved and went back out to the living room. Then her cell phone rang. It was her boyfriend. She lied to him and told him she was somewhere else and would be home soon. We had discussed problems in her relationship with him before, and did so again this evening. That call broke the tension, and she decided she should leave.

That was probably a smart thing to do. As I walked her to the front door, we paused to hug. Then I made my move and kissed her. It was a long and passionate kiss. She felt so good in my arms. She fit just right. Then she left. I thought this was going to be the transition from friends to something more. I pushed for a relationship. She left me a couple of very long messages explaining that as much as she wanted to, she just couldn't break up with him at that time. She also stated that we better cool things off before we made a "mistake." Upset by this news, I tried even harder to win her over.

So one day soon after that, I decided to send her some flowers at work, to express my appreciation for her. I also hoped it would have encouraged her to break up with her boyfriend, so I could replace him. I sent her a dozen yellow roses. The card read: "Without water, these will soon wither. Without love, so will you." Gee, I'm good aren't I? I should have written a book or something. Well, the roses backfired on me. All her co-workers thought they were from him and they kept asking her about them. She fired off an angry e-mail to me, basically telling me to get lost. I responded by trying to apologize, but she replied firmly holding her ground. I was certain that now I had lost her for good. I couldn't understand how or why things had changed so quickly.

Later on, we managed to salvage our friendship, but it was not the same anymore. We were just cordial to one another and that was all. I stopped going to the club, and after that I would occasionally run into her at various places. Each time I would ask her if she was still dating him, and she was. She dated that guy for years. I don't know what she saw in him, but she gave that relationship her all.

I kept her pictures for a long time afterwards, but it was just too cruel to look at them—knowing I had held her in my arms and kissed her so passionately. She's the potential girlfriend who got away. I believe she could have been more than just a girlfriend, if we had only gotten a chance. Not to sound demeaning, but she's one of my favorite fantasies, if not *the* favorite. She's the "bedroom benchmark" whom I measure others against. Only one other woman has come close to her. Oh well, sooner or later we grow up and start chasing after their hearts instead of their asses, anyway. Right, guys?

Material Girl

We met through a mutual friend whom is found elsewhere in this book. She was petite, sexy, and very cute with short blonde hair and a wonderful smile. She dressed impeccably and had lots of friends. She was friendly and personable, but elusive beyond friendship. She was health-conscious, stable, and religious. In other words, she was just about perfect.

Sometimes we would sit together at church. For me, it was special holding a hymnal together and singing side by side. One time, I actually closed my eyes and prayed that someday we would always be together at church. However, that prayer hasn't worked for me yet, with her or anyone else.

Then again, Material Girl liked material things. Sometimes things just weren't good enough for her. She was meticulous in her style and taste. Her materialism reflected her loud and clear. (In other words, she's a lot like me.) She's also particular about her men. I think I actually asked her out on a date early on, but I didn't pass the twenty questions test. Our priorities were different. She wanted things I didn't, but she's been a good acquaintance ever since. We've talked about having lunch together, etc., but it has never panned out. I've also heard that she's a great kisser. (Something else we have in common???)

I've always complimented her when I had the chance, usually through e-mail. Finally, I got brave and jokingly proposed to her one day through e-mail. I haven't heard from her since. I'll try not to make that mistake with the other Trivial Pursuits. I'll just propose to them in person and get slapped like a real man.

Katcher If You Can

She was one of the first people I met in the singles club. My dear friend, Annette, and I were at a private house party one New Year's Eve with a few dozen members. Katcher was a tall woman with a broad face and beautiful eyes. Her lips were broad and stretched from ear to ear when she smiled. She had salt and pepper, shoulder-length hair, and always dressed impeccably. Her figure was more than any man could ever want. She had class and elegance, without having to say or do much. She drew attention and all she had to do was sit back and wait for it to come to her. That must be nice. She was able to break hearts with a single glance. She was very intimidating to me, even though I thought I had outgrown that by now. I didn't necessarily feel that she was out of my league, but rather that I was just not her type. She was a satin sheets type of lady, and I'm more of a bed-in-a-bag kind of guy.

I saw her regularly at these parties and always managed to speak to her, if only to say hello. There was always a line of men vying for her attention. One time, I just got in line along with them. They were trying to impress her with their money. I would watch her out of the corner of my eye. She would examine the men before her, like a lioness stalking out its prey. She was ready to strike upon the most defenseless guy with the fattest wallet. My poor wallet just cringed at the sight of her.

I never asked her out, and I didn't get to know her as well as I wanted to. I did feel that I had one advantage over the other guys with her. I was one of the younger guys at these parties. Most of the others were around their mid-forties to around fifty, I would say. One time, there were two men talking to her at once, bragging about their possessions. They disgusted me. Their stomachs were fatter than their wallets.

My plan was to walk up to her and whisper in her ear, "I'm thirty-eight," and then I would just walk away.

I thought a little reverse psychology might get her attention, but I chickened out. She just remained one of those "what ifs?"

One

Oh, the things a guy will do for a date! Several of us were helping set up for a party at Annette's house one summer afternoon. It was the same group from the singles club. The theme was Hawaiian. As we were setting up tiki torches around the pool, I noticed this cute blonde and introduced myself. She was a little shy, but very nice. We were all in shorts and she had her hair up like most of the other women there. I joked around with her a little, but she was kind of hard to get to know.

After awhile, we had finished setting up and it was time for us to get ready for the party. We walked together to my car, and I told her I wanted to talk with her later that evening. I reached into my pocket to retrieve my cardholder. When I pulled it out, she didn't know what it was at first and jumped. I said I didn't mean to startle her, and proceeded to give her one of my cards.

We all met back at the house about an hour or so later, just before the guests began to arrive. I looked around but didn't see her and thought she was just late or something. I was out by the pool in my best Hawaiian attire as people started to arrive. About that time, a woman came up to me and put her hand on my shoulder.

She said, "Hello," calling me by name.

I said hello back and tried to figure out how I knew this person. She was tall with long blonde hair and wearing a sexy black dress with high heels.

Then it hit me, and I asked, "One, is that you?"

She said, "Yes."

I said, "Oh my gosh, you look great!"

I can't believe I didn't even recognize her. As the saying goes, she cleaned up good!

We talked for a short while, but as others arrived, it was soon apparent that I was going to have stiff competition for her. Well over a hundred people showed up and the evening was great. People were in the Jacuzzi and the pool, and the food was great. I lost track of One as I mingled with other friends and acquaintances. As dusk fell, the announcement came from Annette that it was time for fun and games. There was going to be a dance contest for the men and women and the grand "prize" was a date with the most eligible bachelor and bachelorette. As you might have guessed, on the deck above the pool there stood One and another man, like the prom king and queen. This would be a chance for a guaranteed date with her, so I was ready to go for it. Of course, being a Hawaiian party, the rule was that it had to be a hula dance.

Just great. For the second time in six months, I was about to don a hula skirt and dance in front of a crowd. Except this time it was worse, because I was wearing only swimming trunks and a hula skirt, and pictures were being taken. Only two other men dared to try it with me, so the odds were good. As the crowd roared and cameras flashed, I shook my stuff as best I could. The things we men will do for a date! By the way, those pictures made it onto the club's web site, just in case we weren't embarrassed enough.

To my dismay, I lost. The guy who won turned out to be an asshole, of course. It seems that the prettier the girl, the bigger the jerk they end up with. He bragged about it for the rest of the evening. I didn't get a chance to talk to her much after that. However, not to be defeated, I started flirting with one of the hostesses. She always helped host these parties, but I had never seen her with anyone in particular. She was an older, attractive lady who was a realtor in the area. So I got bold and asked her if she would step outside the gate with me into the yard for a moment. I asked her why she wasn't dating anyone and she said she didn't know. I asked her when was the last time that she had had a date, and her answer was the same. So I asked her when was the last time that she had been kissed, and the answer was still the same.

I said, "Well, that's too long," and I embraced her and gave her a sincere kiss. She was so excited afterwards; she acted like a school kid for the rest of the night.

A week or so later, I gave One a call to see how things were going with the jerk. I don't recall exactly what she said, but I don't think there were any "sparks" between them. Anyway, she was unavailable for me then and in the future. For reasons that are foggy to me now, we never did go out. It was probably another geographical distance thing, but personally I think she had one or more bad experiences with men. Maybe she had even been abused. I don't know. It was just a suspicion from the way she jumped when I retrieved my cardholder. Anyway, she was a pleasure to meet and certainly worth a try. I never did see her again at future parties. But to my surprise, the hostess would certainly give me a big hug and a kiss!

Eyes Only

At one time, she was my landlord, sort of. I had my eyes on her ever since the first time I met her. She was tall with short blondish hair. She had the largest and most incredible green eyes I'd ever seen. They pierced right through you. Her lips were nearly perfect—full and beautifully shaped with a "V" on the center of the upper lip. Her cheekbones were high and her face was a bit broad. She was incredibly feminine with a beautiful figure.

I made a habit of visiting her regularly and eventually we got to know a little about each other personally. She had been married for many years, but her husband was gone a lot. Eventually she confided in me that he had cheated on her more than once. Nonetheless, she was incredibly loyal to him. At one point, he even moved out, but kept coming back.

I would talk to her about anything, just to get to look at her and admire her for awhile. For a long time, she referred to me by a shortened version of my name. I think she did it to tease me. I would remind her that I didn't go by that name. One day she finally said to me: "What would you like me to call you?" I said: "Yours!" She just laughed and went on her way. I confided in her about some relationship issues of my own. I even cried on her shoulder (figuratively speaking) over one of them after we had broken up. She was fiercely loyal and independent. I admired those qualities most about her. After knowing her, and flirting with her for several years, her husband finally left her for good. She had no choice but to divorce him. That was music to my ears.

Then came the day I was moving away. She was only separated at the time, but I decided to confess my feelings toward her anyway. I told her how good things could be for us. She listened but didn't give me anything to go on. I was nervous and my heart was racing. I took her hand and placed it over my heart so she could feel it beating.

I told her, "I can't fake that."

Still, I got no real response. (I thought that was pretty suave of me, and yes, I borrowed it from Midnight.) How dare a woman not fall for my best moves! I can't come up with much more of this stuff, you know. Anyway, I wished her well and tried to encourage her.

Sometime later, I visited her again. She was working alone that day. After another failed attempt to plea for her, I tried one last effort to win her over. On the spur of the moment, I tried to kiss her. She pulled away, stating that she was still "married" and would remain faithful 'til the end. I figured if I ever could win her over, she would be that loyal to me.

Doesn't everyone want someone that loyal? But she was being loyal for loyalty's sake. Her husband didn't earn such faithfulness. She's now officially divorced and I call or visit her about every six months and ask her out. At first, she said she wasn't ready. I didn't blame her for not wanting anything to do with men for awhile. I convinced myself that it wasn't me, but men in general. She was used to being alone most of the time anyway, but I just wanted to be available when she was ready to give it another try.

I think it's a battle of wills at this point. I'm determined not to give up and she's determined not to give in. Maybe she could at least use me for sex and put me out of my misery or something. I don't really care at this point. We'll just have to see how long this story plays out. I'll see you soon, my dear with the beautiful eyes.

Trauma Queen

Be careful what you wish for. You just might get it. On yet another job, she was a co-worker of sorts. I saw her regularly on the job. We hit it off instantly and soon we were dudes of a feather. She was about ten years younger than me. She had long, thick, gorgeous hair. She had pretty eyes and a strong nose. Her skin was exceptionally smooth and healthy looking. Her best "asset" was behind her, and she knew it. We flirted with and teased each other. Her personality was alive and opinionated. She was the type who tackled life for all it was worth.

Then came the Halloween party. Not knowing quite what to expect, I ended up being the only one *not* wearing a costume, of course. Somewhere about the middle of the party, she ran out of film and wasn't able to drive very well. So I volunteered to take her to the store to get some more. We talked and flirted, but she was inebriated. Back at the party, things soon got pretty wild. There was a lot of flashing going on, and women were kissing each other without a second thought. Some were actually doing more than that, to my dismay and delight. I've heard about these kind of parties, but being right in the middle of one was interesting, to say the least.

Before long, and with minimal coaxing, she flashed her best "asset" at me. She had a small tattoo, but I couldn't tell you what it was.

One guy's wife seemed to be the ring leader of this activity, so I asked him what he thought of her behavior. He said he thought it was great. He didn't mind what she did with anyone else; because he knew he would always be the one she came home to in the end (eventually). I stood there beside him for a few moments, watching his wife dance half-naked while people kissed and groped her. To each his own, I guess. The next week, Trauma Queen showed me all the pictures that were taken.

One evening, she invited me over for dinner. She was a great cook, and we had an enjoyable evening with others who were also there. Sometime after that, we went out one night for dinner. It wasn't a date. We just wanted to talk without everyone else around. Then she revealed some personal issues to me. After awhile, I somehow "analyzed" her and told her what I thought she was subconsciously trying to do with her life. She was always so popular and the "life of the party," but underneath, she was crying for help. Tears came to her eyes as she stated that no one had ever been able to recognize her silent pleas before. We sort of bonded that evening, and established a new level of trust and understanding.

Soon after that I was invited to an upcoming holiday banquet. I didn't have a girlfriend at the time and needed a date. Trauma Queen was just the ticket. She anxiously accepted my invitation, and she had just the right dress to wear. A couple of weeks later, on the evening of the event, I went to her house to pick her up. She was stunningly beautiful. I had never seen her with her hair down before. It was incredibly thick, shiny, and full of body. She wore a form-fitting sequined strapless gown. We were late for the event, but I wouldn't have had it any other way. There were several hundred people there, and we just strolled in like the king and queen of the day. It seemed as if everyone stopped and looked at us. We walked right through the middle of the long double lines for the buffet tables. Some jaws dropped and others just stared wide-eyed. I felt so proud to be seen with her. One person asked me if she was a model.

The banquet was very nice. Afterwards, several people came to our table to inquire about us. We told everyone we were just friends, which was true. Afterwards, we decided to go to another restaurant for drinks. We talked more and had a very enjoyable evening. She was one of the best dates I had ever experienced, if not the best—even though it wasn't really a "date."

On the way home, the anticipation was overwhelming. A few blocks before we got to her house, I just stopped in the middle of the road. I leaned over and urgently embraced her and kissed her as passionately as I could. She responded likewise. It was as if we knew this would happen sooner or later, yet we didn't want to ruin our friendship, either. I dropped her off at her house and said goodbye.

It should have ended there, but now we had opened the door of opportunity. It was a matter of when, not if. That opportunity came just a couple of weeks later. She got off work early one evening and needed a ride home. I offered to take her and of course she accepted. We didn't say much along the way. I drove right past the street that led to her house. She didn't say a word. The tiny beads that had torn from her gown weeks before rolled around on the console, emphasizing the silence. We went straight to my place and quickly began to embrace and kiss. We both knew it was inevitable.

There was a moment when we knew we could have stopped it. We just looked at each other for that brief moment, knowing there could be drastic consequences for our actions—life-changing consequences. We knew it was wrong, but we forged ahead, anyway. Why and how these things happen, I still don't fully understand.

We made passionate love that evening. She was very talented and uninhibited. It was an exhilarating experience for both of us. However, it only prompted more questions than answers, and more guilt than excitement. You would think after all I've been through that this was something I could never imagine doing. We were together one more time after that, but I couldn't handle it. I ended our relationship a short time later. I prayed for forgiveness.

She couldn't stay with me very long on that first evening that we had made love. She had to leave. After all, her husband and son had been waiting for her all day to get home so they could open their *Christmas presents.*

Part V: My Friends

In some ways, friendship with the opposite sex is the best love of all. It's genuine and uncomplicated, with little expectations from each other. Our friends carry us through, when others let us down. These are the real success stories in my life.

For comparison, I believe I hit the nail on the head with Date. com. As a widow, her love died intact and unblemished. That's the way I want my love for my friends to remain—no messy divorce, no sorrow, or regret. I have failed at marriage, but have succeeded at friendship. If I remain their friend, that's the way it should stay. The glass is always half full.

Northern Influence

We were just kids—too young to call it love. Still, she is probably more responsible for shaping my view of relationships than anyone else. She was incredibly mature. She was level-headed, patient, and focused. She was a goal to strive for; an example to live by; a glimpse into adulthood. Her childhood forced her into early adulthood. She took care of her younger siblings and in some cases, even her parents. She is probably the reason I was so comfortable with older women later in life and so uncomfortable with women my age. For the longest time (until mid-life), I just couldn't identify with women my age. She knew what she wanted to do at a very young age. I could have strangled her because I had no clue, and even those changed with the seasons.

I can still see her poised against that burgundy velvet wingback chair. The smell of the grand old house is still clear in my memory. It was filled with artifacts from around the world. It had a large stairway with a thick, strong banister. There was even a butler's pantry between the kitchen and dining room. I was a world away when I was there, although it was just across the street. She came down from up north to visit her grandparents every summer for a week or two. Those were some of the best weeks of my life. It's not so much what we did or where we went, but just being together. We bonded early on. She was like a sister to me. I understood her and accepted her. She was smart, practical, and funny. We would share tales of the year's events in our lives. Each summer I saw her, it was as if we had only said goodbye yesterday. She was my first and dearest soul mate. I think she may even have been my first kiss. There weren't any sparks, as I recall, just an experimental sort of thing. I think we knew we were meant to be just friends. We would stay up late just talking on the front porch in rocking chairs.

As the years passed and we grew into teenagers, our bond never wavered. We even introduced some of our friends to each other. We drove the same kind of cars. Ironically, mine was white and hers was black. She went through some family tragedies, and I tried to support her as much as I knew how. However, she changed after the death of one of her siblings. She took life more seriously than she already had before. I could literally envision her descriptions of scenarios as she told them. She was miles ahead of me in maturity. Still, we remained friends. Then we both went away to college.

I was in Florida visiting relatives one time and drove over to a nearby town where she attended college to surprise her. She was in her dorm room talking to her roommate.

Suddenly I just walked in and said, "I'd recognize that damned accent anywhere."

She just sat there on her bed with her jaw open for a moment, and then sprang up to hug me. We went out to dinner and caught up with each other's lives once again. There would be no more visits to the grandparent's house. That was the last time I saw her. I have tried to look her up several times, but didn't really give it an in-depth effort. She became a lawyer, like almost everyone else in her family. I need to see her again. It's been so long. I'm sure we would enjoy "catching up" once again. I'll bet it would seem like we had only said goodbye yesterday.

My Angel

This experience didn't really fit in anywhere in this book, but I decided to share it anyway. This was the only section that was remotely appropriate.

I was working at a department store in a local mall during high school. It was after a co-worker of mine had been killed in a car wreck. Ironically, I would later meet and become close friends with a girl who once dated him. It was a busy weekend night and there was a crowd in my department. I noticed a very distinguished older gentleman standing in the main aisle next to a display. He was wearing an unusual but distinctive suit. He had on a peach-colored shirt with a light gray suit vest and matching slacks. He had white hair that was neatly combed. He complimented a lady who was shopping nearby. He told her how great her hairstyle looked. He was not flirtatious, but he seemed genuinely sincere. She thanked him generously and went on about her shopping. He appeared to be waiting for someone, because of the way he kept looking around.

Meanwhile, there was a line of people at my register. The last person in that line finally came, as I was busy trying to get my register drawer to open. It was stuck for some reason. I was holding several bills in my hand when I looked up to ask if I could help her. There was this beautiful girl standing in front of me. Her eyes were like nothing I had ever seen. They were pure silver—not gray, but mirror-shining sparkling silver. I was shocked to see her at first. I was actually frightened for a moment. I just froze, not knowing what to say or do. She was very kind and asked me something or said something to me, I don't really remember. I don't think she bought anything, but she was looking for her father, or maybe it was her grandfather.

Then she turned and saw him; the distinguished gentleman who had been standing in the aisle. She went to join him and they left together. I watched them until they had walked out the exit door. When I came to my senses, I looked down and the cash that was in my hand was gone. The register drawer was still shut. I tried once again to open it and it opened this time. The cash was in the drawer. I swear I didn't put it there. I couldn't even get the drawer open before I saw her. A chill ran down my spine.

I walked over to the doorway and looked out into the parking lot. The girl and gentleman got into a vehicle and drove away together. Being a guy in high school, I was very interested in cars and knew a lot about most of them. I could even identify most cars at night just by looking at the headlight and parking light configuration in my rear-view mirror. Oddly, I could not identify the vehicle they got into and drove off in. I had not seen taillights like those before. I simply had no idea what kind of car it was. It was like nothing I had ever seen.

I looked down at my hand again where the cash had been, and tried to make sense of what had happened. Eager to tell my co-workers about the experience, I turned around to find them, but no one was around. Strange, I thought. The store was so busy just a few moments before, but now there was no one at all in my department. I walked to the center of the store where the escalators were, still looking for someone—anyone. I got to the center of the store and slowly turned around 360 degrees. There was no one in sight. Not an employee anywhere. No customers. No one. I was there in the middle of a major department store completely alone. Another chill ran down my spine.

I thought I was dead for a moment. I figured I must have died suddenly somehow and this was my afterlife experience. That's when it hit me that she must have been my Angel. She was there to take me from this world. I slowly walked back to my department and sat down. I was dizzy and weak with disbelief. I closed my eyes for a moment and hoped it was all just a dream. When I opened my eyes again and looked up, there were people everywhere—customers and employees. I didn't hear them coming, and don't know how they had time to get there so quickly, but there were people again just like before. I didn't care how they got there; I was just relieved to see people again.

Why and how this experience happened to me, I'll never know. It made a profound impact on my life for the next few years. The only sense I could make of it was that I had a guardian Angel and she had made her presence known to me for some reason. For the next several months, I kept waiting for something to "happen" to me, but it never did. You would think after an experience like that, I would have never gone and done some of the things I've done in my life. Life is funny that way. Maybe she'll be there for me if I ever do need her. Or, maybe I've disappointed her so much by now that she was trying to tell me that was my last chance. Maybe I'll know someday.

Lady Luck

I can't remember how we met. It was right after I was out of high school. We attended colleges that were nearby each other. We started out as friends and had remained close for several years. Her family was cordial to me, and we went out regularly and had a lot of fun together. We worked at different department stores in the same mall in high school. She once dated one of my co-workers who was killed in a car accident, as I mentioned in the previous chapter. We kept in touch through college and beyond. She was pretty and popular. She was ambitious and focused; just the opposite of me. I remember sometimes I would try to talk her into going out, but she would say no if she had to study. She struggled with her weight, but that didn't matter to me. I was supportive of her. I carried a picture of her in my wallet for years.

Her ambition paid off when she landed a great job with a large company after college. I would visit her as often as I could. She was successful and eventually got another job in Florida. I think she went back to school there for her master's degree. I went down to visit her one time during the summer. She had good taste and it was a pleasure complementing her style. One year for her birthday, I bought her the most expensive perfume I could afford. It was $200.00 an ounce (and that was twenty-five years ago). Believe me, I bought less than an ounce.

As time went on, my feelings changed. I was hoping we could become more than friends, but my efforts failed. During one of my overnight visits, I decided to get brave and asked her if she thought we would ever make love. I was still a virgin and wanted her to be my first. She just looked at me and said "no" without hesitation. I was surprised at her answer. She didn't even have to think about it. Talk about disappointment; I was depressed for the rest of the week. We lost touch after the Florida visit. I'm sure she has been successful in all areas of her life.

LA

LA and I were an interesting match. It was an unlikely friendship forged under the common bond of another person through circumstances beyond our control. We despised each other when we first met. She was pretentious and prudish, while I was obnoxious and rude. We warmed up to each other over the years, after we realized we were basically stuck with each other. She married my best friend. It was sort of an "If you can't beat 'em, join 'em" type of deal.

Although we still have strong disagreements, we've grown closer than ever. I can share just about anything with her. I would go as far as to say she's my closest female friend, among several others. I know things about her that she doesn't think I know, and probably vice versa. Mostly what we do is laugh. We can turn almost anything into a joke. I've come to her "rescue" in the night when she was alone, and consoled her through trying times. She has also seen me through my toughest trials. We can do anything together comfortably.

One time we were in the grocery store together and she said to me, "You know, people are going to think you're my husband."

I said, "No, they won't, because we're not arguing."

Only a great friend could joke like that about your marriage.

I've seen her so angry that I've literally cowered in her presence. Also, I've seen her so happy that I'd wish the day would never end. Sometimes it almost feels as if we were the ones who were married. I'm so comfortable in their home, it's like being on vacation (And I usually am when I'm there). Although most of her friends are married, they're really hot, so I like hanging around her to see them, too. She's a cherished part of my life. I hope we continue to be "stuck" with each other from now on.

Annette

We met at a singles party. I told her she looked like Annette Funicello. I thought she would think that was a bad come-on, but she was actually flattered. She had a friendly smile and warm eyes. I was immediately comfortable with her. I don't remember exactly how we decided to stay in touch, but I'm glad we did. She was the first person I met after my divorce.

We visited and went out frequently. I wanted more at first, but she was strong and very wise. She told me I wasn't ready for anything like that, whether I realized it or not. I grew to realize that friendship was the best thing for both of us. We would later share the joys and sorrows of our dating experiences with each other. Although we were never more than friends, we were friends who kissed. This woman boldly told me that I needed to be taught how to kiss—and she taught me, much to my enjoyment. There's an art to it, you know. It's an art, not an act. Once I understood that, she made sure I stayed "up-to-date" on the subject.

One New Year's Eve, I was staying in town at a wonderful hotel that offered one of those package deals. We had dinner there and then went off to a party. It was a wonderful evening, and after midnight we drove back to the hotel. She brought an overnight bag with her, just in case. We went up to the room, and pondered whether we should stay together for the night. She went into the bathroom to change into something "more comfortable." She stayed in there for a very long time. I knew she had doubts, and I wasn't so sure myself. Finally, she emerged in the same clothes she had on before. She had a "please forgive me" look on her adorable face. It was kind of a relief for me, also. She stated that she didn't want to "ruin" the friendship. I took that as a sincere compliment, and drove her home.

The next morning, she came back for brunch, which was also part of the package deal. Afterwards, we left to go see a movie. We were the only ones walking out of the lobby that morning who had to ask each other if they slept well the night before. We had a good laugh over that one. We enjoyed our renewed friendship and had a good day together. There were no regrets. But I couldn't help but try to imagine what might have been.

She once told me that I made her feel safe. That statement had a profound impact on me. Never before had I heard those words. Never before had I felt so much like a man. For that moment, I became all my heroes rolled into one. In return, I felt truly cared for and nurtured by her. It was a beautiful friendship. My dear Annette, how special you have been to me. You have shown me that it takes more courage to care enough to be friends, than to just "leap before you look."

Southern Comfort

She splashed her way into my life one day at the pool. She came on kind of strong at first. It actually scared me for awhile. As I got to know her, I thought she was just like a puppy. She accepts you quickly if you're decent, and can dump you quickly if you're not. She's like a big kid, yet can have some of the most in-depth conversations. She's kind of goofy, yet kind of serious at the same time. She's more interested in what's on the inside than the outside.

Active and social, she needs to be around people. Highly religious and faithful, her heart is as good as gold. She's bright and bubbly and almost always smiling. Eternally optimistic, she'll brighten anyone's day. A caring soul with a good dose of common sense describes her well. Her southern accent, tinged with a little country, makes her all the more adorable.

Our friendship has stood the test of time. Like the others, she's been there for me in sickness and in health; good times and bad. As reliable as the sunrise, she'll be there when you need her. It's truly comforting to know someone like her is there for you, and I'll be there for her also. I hope someone out there will someday love this woman and treat her well.

Lady Bug

Don't let the name fool you. With wicked good looks and a body to match, this woman is a force to be reckoned with. She's fiercely independent and stubborn as a mule. Her body says, "Come and get me," but her eyes say, "Touch me, you S.O.B and I'll turn you into a choir boy." Her heart is guarded tighter than Fort Knox, and I've happily attempted to "break in" over the years. We have a close "cat and mouse" type of friendship. We can say anything to each other. We can curse for no reason at all and just laugh about it. She's almost like one of the guys, but I assure you, she's all woman. She can frustrate me to death, but in some kinky way, I kind of enjoy it.

Somehow, our personalities are an extension of each other. We complement each other well emotionally. I can say or do just about anything around her, without having to think twice or hold back in any way. She gets so excitable around me, sometimes I think she's about to burst. She's always anxious to fill me in on what's been happening in her life. She seems to get herself into predicaments that only we could understand or appreciate. She's definitely a friend for life. We knew it from the start. From the first moment we met, we just knew there was something between us (Well, for me it was lust, but that quickly faded after my best moves didn't even phase her). We have settled into being a part of each other that has bonded us for the long run.

GENIUS

She has an uncanny knack for being in the right place at the right time. That's how she met me, and most of her other friends. Highly opinionated and not afraid to tell you so, Genius is either your friend or your enemy. There's not much in-between. Tall and lanky, she's striking with long blonde hair and absolutely perfect breasts. Her deep voice punctuates her sexuality.

Although she pursued me, she made it clear that she was just "interviewing." Despite my best efforts (well, I guess the disposable tablecloth was a bit tacky), I must have failed the second date interview. Complete with champagne, strawberries, chocolate, and *Rod Stewart's Greatest Hits*, I tried my best to seduce her that night, but nothing happened. What a successful failure! We turned out to be great friends, and that in turn has been one of the best things that ever happened to me. Due to that, she was perhaps the most important date of all.

Knowing her has literally changed my life. She has set me up with many of her friends, who are all gorgeous, by the way. Several of them appear in this book. One of those friends turned out to be the greatest love I've ever known. However, Genius didn't stop there. She is solely responsible for changing my career. In her blunt, uncanny, and analytical way, she told me one day not long after we met, that I was barking up the wrong tree. She told me exactly what I should be doing. She was specific on how to go about it and why I should do it. That was an amazing discovery for me. It was a "light bulb" moment.

I quickly followed up on her advice and soon my life was going in a completely different direction. With renewed confidence and optimism, I was "back in the saddle again." Since men readily identify themselves with what they do for a living, in a way, she renewed my manhood. Genius is near and dear to me, and we have a deep mutual understanding and acceptance between us. I owe her the world, and she's never asked for a dime. I can only repay her by being her friend and believing in her in return. Thank you, Genius, my friend. I'm eternally grateful to you.

In Closing

So what have I learned from these experiences? I've learned that sacrifice and love go hand-in-hand; that rose petals stain tile and sheets; that love stains your heart and mind; and that friends are forever, even if you never see them again. I've learned that love is necessary for life, and not vice-versa. In one form or another, love is forever. It has a life of its own. Some men have a goal or purpose to bed as many women as possible in their life, leaving them hurt. Perhaps my purpose is to love as many women as possible, leaving them healed. Or, maybe I've become the type of guy I've always loathed. Or, maybe I just can't wait until I'm fifty so I can start dating thirty-five-year-olds again!

In case you haven't figured it out, I haven't had the most stable career(s) in my life. Some were prosperous and lasted a good number of years. Some were short-lived, and others were somewhere in-between. I'll even deny ever having some of them altogether (Car salesman? Nah, not me). I've experienced every stage of Maslow's Hierarchy.

My track record with relationships isn't much better. On one hand, I've been in love with two married women and had an affair with a third. On the other, I've given it my all and hopefully it's changed their lives for the better. By far, I'm not the best catch out there, but then again, that is the purpose of this book. It's an average guy's perspective on women and love.

Consciously or unconsciously, maybe my standards are set too high. My wants and my needs seem to conflict. Only one person has been both to me. I say that knowing I've probably shattered any remaining respect I had from her. However, it wouldn't stop me from trying again if the opportunity arose.

The first statement in Part I of this book was that I loved them all, and I still do. I have managed to maintain an intimate relationship with most of my friends and some of the others with whom I've known. I don't mean physically, of course, but close personal relationships. I couldn't stop loving them anymore than I could stop my heart from beating.

Love is like looking in a mirror. Without it, you only see the "good" in yourself because you so readily accept the bad. With love, you can't look at yourself without knowing that the bad is no longer acceptable. Being in love means facing the truth about ourselves. Honestly, we don't deserve it. Isn't it ironic how we can never be good enough for that which we desire the most? So all we can do is simply try. Try to trust. Try to have faith. Always love your friends, and never give up.

I'm a lucky man, indeed.

Printed in the United States
83979LV00004B/145-147/A